The Politics of Postcolonialism

'"If postcolonial studies is to be relevant today," Rumina Sethi argues, "it must become the voice of the people and theorize about movements against globalization, not become part of its grand design." Her critical analysis of the "politics of postcolonialism" and the lack of constructive dialogue with the Marxist perspective, interweaving with analysis of globalization and the state of "postcoloniality," seeks to overcome the academic ossification of concepts that should be integrated with social change and activism.' (Noam Chomsky, Emeritus Professor, Massachusetts Institute of Technology)

'In *The Politics of Postcolonialism*, Postcolonialism and Marxism, too often set in opposition to each other as if they were antagonists or rivals, are joined together in order to forge an activist postcolonial politics. Rumina Sethi challenges postcolonial critics to put their feet back on the ground and to link the postcolonial once again to the political activism by which it has always been inspired. Too often, she suggests, postcolonial studies has advanced as an academic discipline while remaining deaf to the roaring turmoil of global resistance to domination and exploitation. That struggle must continue, and if postcolonial critics are to align themselves with it, Sethi forcefully argues, they must begin by returning to the place where the people dwell.' (Robert J.C. Young, Julius Silver Professor of English and Comparative Literature, New York University)

'This book develops an argument that is both even-handed and radical. Rumina Sethi explores the history and the difficulties of post-colonial theory and without jettisoning its value she urges quite fresh thinking about its political and social implications.' (Dame Gillian Beer, Emeritus Professor of English Literature, University of Cambridge)

The Politics of Postcolonialism

Empire, Nation and Resistance

RUMINA SETHI

First published 2011 by Pluto Press
345 Archway Road, London N6 5AA

www.plutobooks.com

Distributed in the United States of America exclusively by
Palgrave Macmillan, a division of St. Martin's Press LLC,
175 Fifth Avenue, New York, NY 10010

British Library Cataloguing in Publication Data
A catalogue record for this book is available from the British Library

ISBN 978 0 7453 2364 0 Hardback
ISBN 978 0 7453 2363 3 Paperback

Library of Congress Cataloging in Publication Data applied for

This book is printed on paper suitable for recycling and made from fully managed and sustained forest sources. Logging, pulping and manufacturing processes are expected to conform to the environmental standards of the country of origin.

10 9 8 7 6 5 4 3 2 1

Designed and produced for Pluto Press by
Chase Publishing Services Ltd, 33 Livonia Road, Sidmouth, EX10 9JB, England
Typeset from disk by Stanford DTP Services, Northampton, England
Simultaneously printed digitally by CPI Antony Rowe, Chippenham, UK
and Edwards Bros in the United States of America

In loving memory of my mother

CONTENTS

ACKNOWLEDGEMENTS

Most of this book was written during two years of study leave at Oxford and Cambridge as well as the Nehru Memorial Library, New Delhi.

I am grateful to the Panjab University, Chandigarh, for granting me leave without which it would have not been possible to carry out my research. I am also indebted to the Faculty of English, University of Oxford, for inviting me to spend two years in Oxford. I must thank the staff of the English Faculty, the Rothermere American Institute, the Taylorian Institute and the Bodleian library at Oxford, and that of the Nehru Memorial, New Delhi, for assistance in tracing relevant materials. Particular thanks are due to the International Gender Studies Centre, Queen Elizabeth House, University of Oxford; Pembroke College, University of Cambridge; Indian Institute of Advanced Studies, Shimla; the International ACLALS triennial Conference, Hyderabad; and the Rockefeller Centre at Bellagio, Italy, where I presented parts of my work during the course of my research.

My stay at Villa Serbelloni in Bellagio on the salubrious banks of Lake Como during the course of writing this book will always remain the most indelible experience of my research. While on a Rockefeller Fellowship award, I had the opportunity to interact with eminent scholars, poets and thinkers and arrive at new perspectives especially after long discussions over many weeks. I imagined Hannah Arendt, the German philosopher, who had been there decades ago, lazing in the sun and indulging in free conversations on politics, literature and philosophy. Liberalism in politics, the cultivation of the intellect, and keenly standing up for broad and unbridled truth – that was the deep experience I gained there.

Many thanks to Robert Young, Tim Cribb, Catherine Belsey and Kamal Verma who offered valuable suggestions from time to time and gave me their feedback and criticism. Though words are not enough, I am grateful to my dear friends, Rajinder Bhandari, Guinea Singh, Sarah Gracie and Shankar Narayan, for their constant encouragement and unfailing emotional support during a very trying period of my life. Prakash Upadhyaya, Roopinder Singh, Thomas Bisson, Pilar Palacia, Jyoti Sodhi, Meenu Rikhy, Charanjit Singh, Manju and Anil Loona were of immense help whenever I needed them.

I would also like to thank Wolfson College, Oxford, which has always been helpful in matters of accommodation. The days spent here in my old college interacting with scholars from various fields were of enormous value. I would especially like to express my gratitude to the team of publishers at Pluto Press, London, particularly David Castle, Will Viney, Alec Gregory, Judy Nash, Dave Stanford, Sue Stanford and Robert Webb, all of whom have been very patient and always forthcoming with any kind of assistance needed to facilitate my research on this project. Not once did David put excessive pressure on me as I occasionally crossed deadlines even as, in his own inimitable way, he was gently there to remind me of the passing time. Tom Lynton, the cover manager, went painstakingly over every detail of the jacket of this book, always willing to modify and alter. Tim Clark, to whom I am equally indebted, read the manuscript meticulously and uncomplainingly.

To Shelley, I owe a very special thanks for all the scholarly debate and criticism which certainly helped to make this book more incisive and rigorous. I owe him a special debt of gratitude for patiently waiting for me to finish writing as I spent long hours away from him. Finally, I would like to thank my parents: my father who assisted me every inch of the way, who brought me up to be disciplined, determined and rigorous in whatever I did; and my beautiful and ever-supportive mother who made me the person I am and taught me to be intellectually honest. I regret that she never got to see this book completed. I dedicate it to her loving memory.

1

POSTCOLONIALISM AND ITS DISCONTENTS: AN INTRODUCTION

The plenitude of signification is such that 'postcolonial' can indicate a historical transition, an achieved epoch, a cultural location, a theoretical stance – indeed, in the spirit of mastery favoured by Humpty Dumpty in his dealings with language, whatever an author chooses it to mean. (Parry 2004a: 66)

I

In an age replete with innumerable variants of 'post-ist' politics, postcolonialism means so many things to so many people that its full implications necessarily lie outside our grasp. Applied indiscriminately to subjects that would never normally have been perceived collectively, its original focus on colonial politics has now extended from issues of minority-ism under European rule to the hegemony of the US in turning the world global, and from the marginality of women and blacks to the exile of those of us settled outside our nations. Nevertheless, any attempt to withstand and oppose an expansive culture of imperialism will require a form of theoretical polemics that is equally wide-ranging.

For years now, postcolonial theorists have been occupied with finding alternatives to this ill-fitting nomenclature. The term 'postcolonial' has come under a great deal of scrutiny ever since it was used to refer to 'all the culture affected by the imperial process from the moment of colonization to the present day' (Ashcroft, Griffiths and Tiffin 1989: 2). Such an all-embracing definition not only posits colonialism as some sort of continuum with hazy beginnings and no end, not even after a nation's gaining independence, it also places the literatures and politics of practically the whole world within its ambit. Gradually, studies in postcolonialism became preoccupied with all minority cultures – including feminist writing in the third world, black literatures, dalit writing in India, the literature of the diaspora and the dispossessed of the countries of Asia, Africa, Latin America, Australia, Canada, the Caribbean and New Zealand – while also developing an obsessive fixation with stylish, if obscure, theory. In the attempt to 'world' postcolonialism further, Homi Bhabha emphasized border crossing by including 'transnational histories of migrants, the colonized, or political refugees' (Bhabha 1994: 12), whereas Williams and Chrisman advocated the inclusion of 'diasporic communities', ethnic minorities, and of course, the 'formerly colonized national cultures' to widen its ambit (Williams and Chrisman 1993: 373). Ashcroft et al. admitted several essays by African-Americans as 'postcolonial' in their later work, *The Post-Colonial Studies Reader* (1995). With the new imperialism of the superpowers, it seemed that colonialism's obituary had been rather prematurely declared. 'Postcolonial studies' thus became an even bigger discipline than originally envisaged under the older rubric of Commonwealth Literature. Colonialism had never been a metaphor for oppression in such a gargantuan manner.

It was Herder who, in the late eighteenth century, had criticized European subjugation and domination of the globe in his book *Ideas on the Philosophy of the History of Mankind* (1784–91), where eurocentrism was taken to task, especially because of the hegemonic role of European culture through its universalizing tendencies (see Manuel 1968). In order to trace the genesis of postcolonialism, we can return to the notions of 'pluralism' and 'culture' that Herder spoke of, and which finally gave rise to a discipline standing up for marginalized people and their cultures. The idea of postcolonialism as an offshoot of cultural studies perhaps has its origins in this historical development, as the dominant idea of 'civilization' and European 'culture' came to be rejected. For Raymond Williams, too, culture 'was first used to emphasize national and traditional cultures, including the new concept of folk-culture' (Williams 1983: 89). Underpinning of this broad humanistic view was a recognition of Europe's industrial development and its impact on cultures that were 'underdeveloped' in the European sense. The reason why postcolonialism became integral to cultural studies lay in its endeavour to reform the institutions of social democracy by adopting an intellectual and political stance that sought to counter all imperial designs. The analysis of power and of social possibilities thus became part of its cultural agenda.

The institutionalization of postcolonial cultural studies began with assertions of freedom and justice, as in Sartre's preface to Fanon's *The Wretched of the Earth* (1967), or in the anthropological enterprise of writers like Chinua Achebe, who set out to rewrite and revise European accounts of the Maghreb and Africa. The critique of the Enlightenment tradition has never been more incisive than when Sartre quotes Fanon: 'Europe has laid her hands on our continents, and we must slash at her fingers till she lets go ... [L]et us burst into history, forcing it by our invasion into universality for the first time. Let us start fighting; and if we've no other arms, the waiting knife's enough' (Sartre 1967: 11). Prominent spokespersons of the colonized cultures of the world would become the foundational heroes of postcolonialism – figures such as Fanon, who worked for the Algerian resistance movement against France; Césaire, the West Indian poet, his fellow-companion who inspired him; Senghor, later president of Senegal, whose emancipatory statements urged activism among black people; and Gandhi, who led the masses in India to a non-violent revolution against the British. Their best-known literary descendants today are Edward Said, Gayatri Spivak and Homi Bhabha, whose writings and commentaries are regarded as intrinsic to what is known as colonial discourse analysis. Significantly, the inclusion of the cultural effects of colonialism within postcolonial studies becomes apparent by the late 1970s, when 'post' begins to signify more than simply the historical passing of time. This coincides with the publication of Said's *Orientalism* (1978), which dealt with issues of colonial representation and cultural stereotyping.

Following decolonization struggles across the world, the power of the US grew phenomenally, as did the legitimacy of the monopoly of reason appropriated by institutions like the International Monetary Fund and the World Bank. Postcolonial studies, at this point, is regarded to have exhibited a marked complicity with the market economy by not making neoliberalism its target. Liberal capitalism, for its part, contributed a great deal to undoing the borders of nation-states with the global spread of multinational corporations. With the growth of market capitalism, postcolonial studies appeared to have a duality of purpose: the promotion of revolutionary pedagogy along with an inbuilt critique of nations and nationalisms as cultural constructions. The demise of the nation, if only in the text-books, carried the risk of removing the very sentiment revolutionaries had fought for. As a discipline, postcolonial studies, rather than pioneering a focus on historical Marxism underpinned by popular struggles of dissent in the third world, began to scrutinize the cultural aspects of issues of race, gender, class and, of course, the nation. Theory, as such, would undoubtedly remain an abstraction unless its proponents succeeded in applying it to concrete instances of economic and social exploitation, or at least in fashioning an agenda replete with acts of resistance to western-dominated discourses.

Among academics, the decline of the nation and the corresponding expansion of the metaphor of marginalization has led to the embrace of concepts like diaspora, hybridity, difference and migrancy – concepts that are all related to the growth of the global economy and have come to be seen in terms of new configurations of dominance. The prioritizing of global capitalism over praxis corresponds to the waning of Marxism and Marxist studies. While there are obvious limits to what literary studies can accomplish in relation to changing the new economic and political realities, the prescriptions of the latter have been imposed, consciously or unconsciously, and hegemonically, through the global pressure to fashion a university curriculum that blunts postcolonial sensibilities. If social, economic and political concerns are to remain at the heart of postcolonial studies, it will need to struggle continuously against the crises introduced by rapidly changing teaching practices as much as by the rising cosmopolitanism of the world.

It is thus that postcolonialism has acquired a whole new range of meanings today, as it moves away from addressing imperial control to servicing neocolonialism. Since 'colonialism' is really an anachronistic term for capital expansion, it comes as no surprise that contemporary capital expansion through processes of globalization is often referred to as 'neocolonialism'. Although globalization can be defined as the creation of global markets, it is also a practice involving the search for low-cost labour (Wallerstein 1983: 39). The capitalist market has now travelled to the 'point of production' in tandem with seeking out a cost-effective labour force that will re-export manufactured goods back to the home country (Childs and Williams 1997: 6). Among postcolonialism's many connotations, one interpretation stands out in the contemporary milieu – that it has less significance as denoting 'after colonialism' than in emphasizing the persistence of colonial tendencies in terms of a continuing imperialism.

Postcolonialism finds itself in a particular predicament today: it purports to be a liberatory practice but it remains nevertheless coeval with modes of oppression, particularly after its appropriation within the United States' university curricula. Its crisis results from its origins having been both political and historical – postcolonialism emerged out of struggles against colonization, and being part of that history it is grounded in confrontation with authority and aggression. Today, however, the end of European subjugation does not imply the end of the existence of western superpowers with their neocolonial tendencies. The increasing pressures of the west have led to the institutionalization of postcolonial studies in universities all over the world. This means that while it is no doubt still seen as a subversive discipline, it is also perceived to be implicated in western hegemony, all the more so given its compatibility with other contemporary theoretical approaches such as those of postmodernism and poststructuralism.[1]

Correspondingly then, pressure has been placed on postcolonial studies to illustrate its usefulness in the context of globalization against apologists for the free-market economy, as well as to take a passionate stance for the defence of the marginalized and the powerless. Viewing the current condition of global capitalism and the rise of the 'new' imperialism from the point of view of postcolonial writing, one is confronted by issues that draw attention to the fact that what began as a deeply versatile discipline for introducing more activism into the academy, ended up in mere codification therein, creating a schism between 'postcolonialism' and 'postcolonial studies'. The different implications of these terms will be elaborated upon later in the chapter, but suffice it to say here that the former is taken, in this book, as referring to a condition of living, a practice, a political belief or set of political beliefs that come into effect in a situation of oppression or marginalization, and that can help counter that oppression through protest, resistance and activism. The latter term, by contrast, underpinned as it is by 'postcolonial theory', is a discipline that was set up to examine the literature of political protest and resistance among people of the third world, but which has come to represent university curricula abounding in issues of hybridity and multiculturalism as these are taught in elite institutions of the world. The two – postcolonialism and postcolonial studies – have largely been mixed up in academic criticism, adding to the confusion. Most academic analyses use the former in place of the latter.

So, what are the *politics* of postcolonialism? By the 'politics of postcolonialism', I do not intend to indicate governmental functioning or the process of state-building, but the different agendas that the former colonized countries employ in resolving their identity crises by combating and intervening in the legacies of imperialism and neocolonialism, be it in terms of nation-formation or even enthusiastic forays into trade and stock exchange controlled by the west. In other words, politics here stands for both resistance strategies as well as comprador advantages. The term 'politics' is increasingly important when tracing the connections between postcolonialism, nationalism and globalization, areas covered in this book. By widening the term 'politics' in the world we inhabit today, we can envisage the former colonies as constituting the neocolonial empire of the United States (and to some extent, Europe), giving a new twist to the earlier implication of the term, which, as it takes on implications of global give and take, economic hegemony, and the rise of a new kind of diasporic identity, makes it necessary to interrogate the growing power of the United States. By pursuing these implications, the present book aims to introduce new readers not only to the meaning and nature of postcolonialism, but, more importantly, to its contemporary manifestations and its close engagement with globalization.

'Postcoloniality', which would be the state or the condition of being postcolonial, is itself not an unproblematic term any longer. Since the word 'politics' is laden with multifarious meanings and nuances, the postcolonial critic must try to find an equation between the critique of postcoloniality and its liberatory potential, arriving thereby at a 'politics' capable of working for the entire constituency of postcolonial scholars and critics. The variants of postcolonialism along with their particular agendas can be taken up by identifying their differences from the Marxist approach. Marxism as praxis can be differentiated from postcolonialism as textualism by following Aijaz Ahmad's distinction between the two as outlined in his book *In Theory* (1993). My discussion here, in very broad strokes, turns and overturns the terrain of early postcolonial theory and its chief proponents from a Marxist perspective to expose the contradictions and paradoxes within which postcolonialism operates in the academy. Although Marxism has been hugely discredited, it has not been possible to shrug off its reservations about postcolonial studies. The Marxist critics of postcolonial studies, who bemoan its closeness to poststructuralism, narrate the histories of colonialism, decolonization and freedom struggles, keeping in mind the all-important part played by the people. Its critics – Ahmad and Dirlik are particularly vociferous in this regard – would like postcolonialism to be an instrument of people's politics. The postcolonial practitioners, for their part, consider postcolonialism as a necessary intervention in the dominant discourse of European humanism which stretches into contemporary globalism. What is common to both views is the platform across which their critical commentaries are mounted – that postcolonial thought as well as Marxism are eurocentric, having originated in the western academy. Unfortunately both Marxism and postcolonial studies maintain a distance from each other to their mutual cost.

The academic manifestations of postcolonialism, predominantly postcolonial theory and postcolonial studies, have been criticized for developing right-wing tendencies and severing links with what was taken to be their responsibility following decolonization struggles – namely, to maintain an adequate historical representation of the condition of the formerly oppressed and support the creation of an equitable, anti-eurocentric world through public-spirited debate rather than textual obscurantism. Despite the disconcerting nature of postcolonial studies, nowhere do I imply that it has reached the end of the road, as several critics have stated over the last decade, even though a reconceptualization of postcolonialism is on the cards in the context of increasing globalization.[2] One significant concern here is to offer some kind of defence against accusations of eurocentrism and location politics, which I attempt later, to level the battlefield so that we might make room for further discussion on the direction postcolonial studies can take in the future.

Postcolonial studies has received its strongest criticism for its alleged 'metaphysics of textualism' (to use San Juan's expression in his analysis of Bhabha and Spivak) that 'void[s] the history of people's resistance to imperialism, liquidate[s] popular memory, and renounce[s] responsibility for any ethical consequence of thought' (San Juan 1998: 22). Postcolonial identities cannot be recuperated by recounting cases of ambivalence or the simultaneous presence of sameness and difference, but by emphasizing historically specific acts of resistance. These 'acts' could be those of movements resisting colonial powers, of national integration movements, or acts of resistance to new imperial controls over recklessly globalizing economies. Postcolonial studies, by addressing representations of alterity and the ambivalent relations between centre and periphery, tends to lose its historical-material reality and begins to reproduce itself in purely theoretical terms. As theory, comprising strategies of reading and textualism, sweeps aside the political expression of a transformative history, silencing the subalterns who need more than ever to speak, postcolonial studies leads to a marked disappointment among exponents of Marxism as it begins to rely more and more on poststructuralist methodologies. Bhabha's idea of the self-as-other and the other-as-self – both of which serve to make colonialism a very problematic category in which 'slippage', 'excess' and 'difference' between binaries cannot be easily dismissed (Bhabha 1994: 86) – has provoked his critics to ask how, if it can be perceived only as a process of rapidly eroding self-images, identity can be visualized at all. Where would one locate the politics of struggle and resistance which are necessary parts of decolonization movements?

Outside the generalized academic pronouncements concerning hybridization, local struggles continue in their specificity, while inside the academy, national identity and native locations are well-nigh lost. By its very dismissal of foundationalism, postcolonial studies loses sight of the world of real events such as those real national struggles, and of local identities which it benefits every nation to preserve.[3] There arises, thus, an increasing rift between postcolonial *theory* on the one hand, which forms the vanguard of postcolonial studies, and what can be called postcolonial *practice* on the other. The former is underwritten by the 'high' theory of Derrida, Lacan and Foucault, incorporated by their disciples in the academy (especially Said, Spivak and Bhabha), and the latter espoused by a host of other critics who condemn the encroachment of French theory into postcolonial criticism (see Moore-Gilbert 1997: 1). The disavowal of real struggles has become so suspect that those who insist that terms such as 'nationhood', 'Marxism', 'citizenship', 'constitutionality' and 'revolution' are acceptable even today are curiously not called 'postcolonial' critics even as they inhabit a postcolonial world.[4] Indeed, the only critics deemed to be 'postcolonial' are those who are also 'postmodern' (Ahmad 1995a: 10). The divide between postcolonial theory and postcolonial practice has, further, bred a polarization between academics who work in the third world and those who have migrated to the west. The 'original' postcolonial theorists like Spivak and Bhabha are now considered to have been 'appropriated' by the global economy and judged inauthentic in terms of the problems they purport to represent as they have moved westward; those who are left behind then claim to be the 'genuine' practitioners. However, many of the latter have consciously chosen to keep a safe distance from 'the postcolonial', which is now regarded as a compromise with colonialism amounting to a kind of western 'academic imperialism' (Paranjape 1996: 43).[5] An uneasiness has also crept in as a result of the variety of intellectuals, from Edward Said to Lata Mani, all of whom describe themselves as 'postcolonial'.[6] The fashioning of postcolonial identities that betray an excessive reliance on western theory, promoted by intellectuals commanding positions of power in the western academy, creates a paradigm of the colonial relationship which approximates to centuries of colonial rule.[7]

Two significant, and much discussed, points of contention concern postcolonial theory's arcane discourse of hybridity and its sweeping use of anti-essentialism, both of which I will briefly discuss here before turning to my main concern as it relates to the theory's embrace of globalization and dissociation from the nation. The language-centric theories of cultural translation articulated by Bhabha, who is considered to be postcolonialism's 'most doctrinaire instigator', and the ventriloquism of Spivak who builds upon voiceless subalterns, have been deplored for blunting the sensibilities of many thinking people across the third world – which is precisely what keeps postcolonialism from becoming a collective with a mass base (San Juan 1998: 25, 30).[8] Take, for example, the following lines from Stuart Hall:

> Hybridity, syncretism, multidimensional temporalities, the double inscriptions of colonial and metropolitan times, the two-way cultural traffic characteristic of the contact zones of the cities of the 'colonised' long before they have become the characteristic tropes of the cities of the 'colonising', the forms of translation and transculturation which have characterised the 'colonial relation' from its earliest stages, the disavowals and in-betweenness, the here-and-theres, mark the *aporias* and re-doublings whose interstices colonial discourses have always negotiated and about which Homi Bhabha has written with such profound insight. (Hall 1996: 251)

This is Hall's defence of both hybridity and Bhabha's vocabulary. Hall's writing is otherwise insightful, like that of many other postmodern theorists, displacing the notion of universality and homogeneous identities in the new global cultural world, and dismissing the binaries of self and other that can never exist as closed systems of identification. Following the Derridean notion that there will be always something 'left over', Hall argues that identities can never be defined by 'essence or purity', but are constituted by an acknowledgment that they live 'with and through' difference and not despite it (Hall 1990: 230, 235). Bhabha's concepts of hybridity and ambivalence similarly indicate the dismembering of fixed and 'pure' categories which is a symptom of the borderless world we live in (see Bhabha 1994). But couched in a quagmire of jargon, postcolonial studies falls short of its transformative and transgressive potential. Gilroy's 'double consciousness' that breaks free of exclusiveness and ethnicity inherent in the claims of nationhood, that increasingly aligns itself with 'creolisation, métissage, mestizaje, and hybridity', propagates the same message in equivalent expressions (Gilroy 1993: 1, 2).

Marxists have not only targeted theories of hybridity floated in obscure prose but have also criticized the other key postcolonialist notion: 'anti-essentialism'. Where the former dispenses with categories and, more precisely, locations, in the service of ambivalence, thus valorizing a fluid relationship between the colonizer and the colonized, the latter, which is inspired by postmodernism, takes away what one is fighting for. It cannot be denied that Spivak's advocacy of anti-essentialism as a theoretical concept is rather over-stretched. Bit by bit, she dismisses every facet of an identity politics, including perceptions of the subaltern and the proletariat as being 'disenfranchised' (Spivak 1990: 103). Thus dealt with, peasant movements, national struggles and agitations, loyalties and sacrifices became part of 'comprador' politics.[9] Critics claim that the poststructuralist methodology Spivak employs is politically impotent, since anti-essentialism and the idea of origins as myth foreclose the very fact of the subaltern's history.[10] It is, then, not unreasonable to argue along with Dirlik that 'postcolonialism', 'rather than a description of anything, is a discourse that seeks to constitute the world in the self-image of intellectuals who view themselves (or have come to view themselves) as postcolonial intellectuals' (Dirlik 1994: 339). Notably, Dirlik does not make a distinction between postcolonialism and postcolonial studies but substitutes one for the other. Along with the subaltern voice, anti-essentialism also takes away any belief in the nation as a safeguard for its citizens, even though it is to the nation that the underprivileged will appeal for protection when faced with adverse circumstances. Hardt and Negri's argument concerning the supersession of the nation-state by Empire augments those anti-essentialist readings that obfuscate the very idea of resistance, struggle and even of the people (see Hardt and Negri 2000).

By far the most important charge, particularly in the context of this book, is the allegation that the relationship between postcolonialism and global capitalism has been left unexamined by almost all postcolonial critics, and that postcolonial studies, as a consequence, propelled by the metropolitan methodology of postcolonial theory, has developed side by side with the growth of neocolonialism. Swept up as it has been by the wave of western poststructuralism, it is claimed that 'postcolonialism' fails to counter imperialism in the guise of its new avatar, globalization, and as a result tends to conflate the local experiences of particular countries with a sweeping postcolonial sensibility acquired by postcolonial theorists as they migrate to centres of the global corporate world (Dirlik 1994: 340). Thus narrow and individual experiences get translated into interpretations that seemingly resonate with globalism. That postcolonial intellectuals, furthermore, promote 'multiculturalism' and 'cultural hybridity' is taken as a sign of complicity in sponsoring postcolonial corporatism. In the United States, postcolonial studies is evidently related to the growing ascendancy of a cultural studies programme and the advancement of the US as a global power by the end of the Cold War. The idea of 'postcoloniality' in cultural criticism is concurrent with the emergence of global capitalism. The implications of 'postcolonial', in this sense, are threefold: it is a concrete reference to conditions prevailing in countries that were formerly colonized; it is the condition of globality following colonialism; and it is a discourse or academic discussion of the conditions of colonialism and global capitalism (Dirlik 1994: 331–2). There is a confusion of these three interpretations in our understanding of the postcolonial, especially with increasing globalization when the term 'third world' gives way to 'postcolonial', replacing our understanding of the former as designating those areas and peoples that belong to neither the first nor the second world. As 'third world' becomes displaced by 'postcolonial', the politics of location as well as that of identification are confounded.[11] It may be inferred from such an understanding that postcolonial intellectuals are those who not only 'produce the themes that constitute postcolonial discourse' but, more importantly, are those who participate in the discourse of postcolonialism rather than actively pursue third-world concerns (Dirlik 1994: 332). Postcolonialism as a discursive construction, freed from its third-world location, is then easily transferred across the Atlantic to reside in the classrooms of advanced capitalist countries that have a homegrown postcolonial population of their own, made up of ethnic groups and migrants.

As postcolonialism travels, it breaks the rigidity of categories such as east/west, self/other and so on, a cause for great excitement and good cheer for many like Gyan Prakash as the third world bursts open its territories and penetrates the 'inner sanctum of the first world', 'arousing, inciting, and affiliating' with its subordinated groups such as the 'socialists, radicals, feminists, minorities' (Prakash 1990: 403). The disaffiliation with the third world, taken as a territory or a location, not only releases postcolonialism from its commitment to anti-eurocentrism, it also marks a change in its orientation as third-world identity begins to reside in traces and transitions, diaspora flows and migrancy. Having become global in its conceptualization, the 'third world' becomes a cultural category of western academic criticism, thus making the distinction between postcolonial theory and postcolonial practice even more marked.[12] The third world, which was once a place where radical alternatives to the first world were available, develops contagion with the latter in its global give-and-take, leading Ahmad to say, though less spiritedly than Prakash, that 'we live not in three worlds but in one' (Ahmad 1993: 103).

It is indeed difficult to reconcile postcolonialism's anti-eurocentric function of tearing down western culture's totalizing perspective through the interrogation of orientalist stereotyping, the representations of history, the hegemony of English studies, and gender and racial constructions on the one hand with the celebration of multiculturalism and diffusion manifested in postcolonial studies on the other. One effect of the latter interpretation is the ease with which the United States and Canada have become postcolonial. Yet those who live and practice in the 'real' postcolonial world are seldom part of the rubric of postcolonial studies. It excludes separatist groups killing each other in the name of preserving homogeneity; the seductions by modern capitalism of nationalist societies that are unwittingly implicated in globalization processes; diasporic intellectuals of the so-called third world settled in the west whose 'postcolonial' leanings are ambiguous such that they belong nowhere and everywhere; and even the extremely radical politics of the subaltern studies historiography focused on class struggles. While postcolonial studies as a discipline flourishes with abandon within academia, in the world outside, postcolonialism 'shows in murderous ethnic conflict, continued inequalities among societies, classes, and genders' (Dirlik 1994: 347). The 'postcolonial' has also been deemed ineffective because the postcolonial generation has now forgotten the *Sturm und Drang* of the actual period of colonization.

An even more devastating effect of the 'hybrid' version of contemporary postcolonial studies has been its utter neglect of the people. It is this that has led to the charge of a collaborative intent between postcolonialism and globalization. In this context, Miyoshi is provoked to write:

> We witnessed a full-scale genocide in Rwanda as the world stood by. Many areas in the former colonies in Africa, Eastern Europe, the Middle East, Central America, the Indian Subcontinent, and possibly inland China, in short a vast majority of the world, are threatened with unmediated disorder resulting from overpopulation, poverty, and civil violence. Forsaken by

> the industrialized elites as unprofitable, the majority of humanity faces a bleak future. As we talk about postcoloniality and postindustrialism in metropolitan academia, we ignore those billions outside our ongoing discourse for whom life has nothing 'post' about it. (Miyoshi 1997: 54)

In the same spirit, San Juan lists the aborigines in the Americas, the New Zealand Maoris, the child prostitutes in India, Thailand and other countries, the plight of the refugees in Africa, Chechnya, the erstwhile Yugoslavia, the Mayan Indians, the people of East Timor, and so on, and questions the commitment of postcolonial studies to the representation of the underprivileged of the less advanced countries of the world:

> Where were the postcolonial gurus during the Gulf War? What is their stand on political prisoners like Mumia Abu Jamal, Elizam Escobar, Leonard Peltier, and many others languishing in U.S. jails? ... How does postcolonial theory ... explain the plight of millions of 'overseas contract workers' – women domestics, 'hospitality girls', and mail-order brides comprise this large, horizontally mobile cohort – all over the world? (San Juan 1998: 13)

San Juan calls postcolonialism a client of the imperialist machinery and illustrates his argument by citing two case studies, that of Rigoberta Menchú of Guatemala and Maria Lovena Barros of the Philippines. The United States, which has enormous investments in Guatemala such as the United Fruit Company, is known for its exploitation of the Mayan Indians who constitute 60 per cent of the population but live on plots 'the size of a grave' (San Juan 1998: 32). Ninety-eight per cent of Guatemala's land is owned by some 150 elite companies, many of which have collaborated in various ways with the CIA. Episodes from the life of Rigoberta Menchú are well known. Having witnessed the murders of her parents and brother – dubbed guerrillas and terrorists by the US supported government of Guatemala – Menchú narrates the story of her commitment to the indigenous people's struggle in her book *I, Rigoberta Menchú*. Hers is a narrative of survival, a link between the personal and the public which serves as the inverse of the 'hyperreal, labyrinthine discourse from the metropole' (San Juan 1998: 36). Menchú's memoir may be a personal utterance but it has universal resonance in that it unites people struggling for peace, egalitarianism and honesty at the level of commitment to humanitarian values. In the concluding lines of her memoir, Menchú writes:

> I've travelled to many places where I've had the opportunity to talk about my people. Of course, I'd need a lot of time to tell you all about my people, because it's not easy to understand just like that. And I think I've given some idea of that in my account. Nevertheless, I'm still keeping my Indian identity a secret. I'm still keeping secret what I think no-one should know. Not even anthropologists or intellectuals, no matter how many books they have, can find out all our secrets. (Menchú 1984: 247)

The 'secret' that she conceals is a measure of her struggle and resistance which cannot be academically textualized despite her confessions. What San Juan purports to do is imbue Menchú with an ethnic substance or aboriginal identity which is dismissed in deconstructive criticism. He uses words like 'rooted', 'distinctive', 'inviolate', 'subjecthood' and 'enfranchisement' (San Juan 1998: 38, 50) to signify that Menchú's – or for that matter, Guatemalan – identity cannot be desacralized or undermined by the logic of a postcolonial science.

The life of Maria Barros – who founded the women's organization in the Philippines known as Makibaka (Movement of New Nationalist Women) – once again opposes 'postcolonial eclecticism and ambivalence' (San Juan 1998: 44). During the 1970s, Filipino women were compelled to earn their subsistence through servicing the US troops who had established military bases in the Philippines during the Marcos dictatorship – 'hospitality trade', 'mail-order brides' and 'warm body export' were terms euphemistically used for flesh trade in the same way as 'comfort women' was used to refer to Korean women who served as sex slaves for Japanese troops during the Second World War. As Barros began to activate peasant women and those working in factories by initiating reforms, she realized that the primary difficulty was that of convincing middle-class women that they were being exploited. She was imprisoned in 1974 but managed to escape soon after, devoting herself wholeheartedly to the poor and the needy, thereby sacrificing 'the luxury of claiming an oxymoronic, shifting, and plural identity expressed in tropes of positional/border identities' (San Juan 1998: 49). In 1976, Barros was killed in an encounter. At that time, she was only 28. If Barros's broken, dead body becomes a symbol of the substantive real, a powerful figure of committed feminism, the dead body of the woman who has immolated herself on the pyre of her husband represents subaltern silence in postcolonial studies (Spivak 1988b).[13] Which of the two is more real? Spivak's concept of the silenced subaltern is more conceptual and interpretive than real, tending to become extremely disturbing for those who are involved in the retrieval of subaltern voices (Loomba 1993: 218).

And what of El Sa'adawi's prostitute, Firdaus, another of San Juan's examples (1998: 101–3), who kills a foul-mouthed and coarse pimp and is scheduled to die at the end of the novel, *Woman at Point Zero*? Can she challenge the very concept of the 'unspeakable' subaltern? Firdaus, whose character is based on a woman El Sa'adawi encountered in Qunatir Women's Prison where she herself was imprisoned by the Sadat government in 1981, has a narrator to communicate the events of her life:

> I saw her walk out with them. I never saw her again. But her voice continued to echo in my ears, vibrating in my head, in the cell, in the prison, in the streets, in the whole world, shaking everything, spreading fear wherever it went, the fear of the truth which kills the power of truth, as savage, and as simple, and as awesome as death, yet as simple and as gentle as the child that has not yet learnt to lie.
>
> And because the world was full of lies, she had to pay the price. (El Sa'adawi 2007: 114)

There could be no more fitting testimony to the power of the subaltern voice than what Sa'adawi evokes in her novel. Among the many examples of the speaking subaltern, that of a nineteenth-century Indian *bhadramahila*, Rassundari Devi, who, despite her high caste, was removed from school in order to enter into an early marriage, deserves recognition.[14] Even in those times, subversions against the dominant order existed in the form of popular songs and lullabies which played upon the miseries of married life that separated young daughters from their mothers and playmates. After her marriage, Rassundari had to learn to read and write in secrecy through a recollection of the alphabet from her son's school textbooks (Sarkar 2001:127). Despite household chores and the demands of her several children, she succeeded in writing *Amar Jiban* (My Life), the first autobiography ever to be written by a Bengali woman. A careful reading of this text uncovers the transgressions, the desire for freedom and the misery of having to bring up children (quite contrary to the Indian ethos in which offspring are regarded as a blessing from the gods).

Against such encounters with speech and subversion, postcolonial studies, having arrived at the metropolis, appears to be at variance with social change and uninformed by activism. There is also the perplexity of dealing with an anti-foundationalist sensibility that continues to denigrate nation and race as homogenizing concepts and structures even where they might, in fact, offer the promise of liberation from the hegemonizing west. Contemporary western theory is considered to be the primary villain here, as responsible for the growing disconnection from political activism and the prioritizing of text over context (see Ahmad 1993: 3). Further, the privileging of colonial discourse or reading practices that favour migrant fictions tends to dismiss the task of 'writing back', and, in the process, fails to address the contribution of regional literatures. *The Vintage Book of Indian Writing* by Rushdie and West is a case in point: no writers excepting Sadat Hassan Manto can qualify as 'Indian' unless they write in the metropolitan language, English. Postcolonial studies thereby becomes the new agenda of a west that has not only sold its theory to the former colonies but also appropriated resistance so completely as to make it part of its own past and present. This explains the adversarial attacks that see postcolonial studies as part of the project of the eurocentric academy.

Marxists and postcolonial theorists have not been the best of friends. Where the former privileges actual historical struggles between two unevenly matched sides, the latter is hostile to this reductive vision, promoting instead the mutual contagion of binary entities. The logic of Marxist ideology is the presence of 'material unevenness' and the need to resist exploitation; the postcolonial approach is culturalist, emphasizing 'the intermixing of cultures' such that we may never be able to distinguish the exploiter from the exploited (Bartolovich 2000:140). Recourse to binary oppositions to identify the enemy may be one way of ensuring resistance and struggle, but postcolonialists also have a point when they claim that interpreting struggles on the basis of such oppositions can contribute in removing politics altogether rather than politicizing the situation. To define the postcolonial in terms of cut-and-dried closed categories would amount to doing a great disservice to the interplay of politics and power relations in any given situation. Postcolonial approaches thus pose a powerful challenge to dependency theories – which view underdevelopment as a result of the exploitation of the 'peripheries' by the wealthy 'core' countries – by suggesting that the colonizer–colonized relationship is a two-way street, since the contamination of both cultures is mutual. This is an extremely valuable insight which allows a glimpse into the intricate ways in which a colonizing culture is affected by what it does outside its territory.[15] The Gulf War of 1990–91, for example, which was generally seen in terms of the 'clash of civilizations' thesis, would not be visualized so simplistically through the postcolonial lens. The war was a consequence of western interests in middle-east oil reserves as much as Saddam Hussein's atrocities towards the Kurds and others and a myriad other unsaid and unstated reasons. For Hall, the Gulf War, 'in which *both* the crisis of the uncompleted struggle for "decolonization" *and* the crisis of the "post-independence" state are deeply inscribed', may thus be described as a 'classic "post-colonial" event' which is ambiguous at best (Hall 1996: 244).[16] But despite the effects of contamination, the nationalist urge remains directed towards unconditional freedom and pure origins. A quick glance at the speeches of Nehru or Nkrumah will dispel the academic beneficence of cultural translation. Who can deny the power politics that still exist in the world between India and Britain, Grenada and the United States, or Palestine and Israel? Can India, Grenada or Palestine exist comfortably in the knowledge of mutual contagion? The global interchange between

China and India notwithstanding, the slightest build up of arms on the Indo-China border immediately summons up the categories of 'us' and 'them', even as Indian and Chinese academics write their scholarly articles on the 'transnational' politics of postcolonialism.

II

In sum, there are primarily two related objections Marxists have against postcolonial studies: the eurocentric agenda and location of its proponents and the displacement of activism in its conception. Instead of originating in the third world, postcolonial studies has flourished in Britain, Australia, Canada, New Zealand and now the United States. To say that postcolonialism has become a first-world discourse is not entirely off the mark: it did impact the western academy in a big way, concerned as it was with issues of imperialism, nation, race, empire, diaspora and minority cultures. Postcolonial studies rapidly became a booming discipline with new centres and institutions opening up in western universities alongside a glut of journals and conferences with special focus on postcolonialism.

Yet, as it turned out, the term 'postcolonial' came to be applied to such different historical circumstances in locations utterly distinct from one another, suggesting the formation of multifarious identities and a variety of methodologies, that flexibility became its strength as much as its weakness. A string of critical commentaries from the late 1980s and the 1990s illustrate this trend.[17] Postcolonial studies, in its borrowings from post-structuralism, did not stop with the critique of eurocentrism but struck severe blows to notions of identity, history and nation, and to world-system theories that had relied excessively on a linear conception of modernization ushering in globalization. Marxism's inability to deal with these pressing issues allowed postcolonial studies to take over the mantle of an empowering discipline in its place.[18] When a culturalist challenge was introduced in the face of Marxism's materialist explanation of the colonial state's journey into modernity, aided by Bhabha's 'cultural differences' (Bhabha 1994: 140) and Hall's idea of the transcendentalism of global culture (Hall 1996: 247), Marxists cried foul, calling postcolonialism unhistorical and detecting a hidden agenda of furthering eurocentrism.[19] The importance of the nation and of historical agency, which alone could answer back to the ongoing eurocentrism of rapid capital expansion and neocolonialism, was emphasized by the Marxists even as postcolonial theorists disavowed such factors.

Considering the arguments of both camps, it becomes evident that we cannot afford to neglect the nation, its citizenry, or for that matter, historical agency, which once again brings postcolonial practice head to head with postcolonial studies. A more nuanced approach that reaches far beyond the categories delineated by Bhabha and Spivak should become the framework of postcolonial studies. In order to steer it more towards practice, a grafting of postcolonialism onto Marxist principles can help us arrive at an understanding of both structures of power and the means of resistance. Instead of rejecting Marxist criticism, an effort should be made to expose the other side of postcolonialism, an approach that still has relevance for third-world societies and popular struggles, and which remains connected with the problems that emerged from the colonial encounter. As an advocate of the practice of postcolonialism, Young dismisses the charge of eurocentrism by arguing that while postcolonial studies may have flourished in the west, postcolonialism itself is very much a product of the east and, correspondingly, postcolonial intellectuals outside the west are not hegemonically receptive to globalization and capital inflows (Young 2001). Several postcolonial theorists and philosophers of poststructuralism – Fanon, Memmi, Bourdieu, Althusser, Lyotard, Derrida, Cixous – came from or were connected with Algeria, an unacknowledged relationship with the east that must not be disregarded, and that should lay much criticism regarding the western origins of postcolonialism to rest (Young 2001: 413).[20] Although a German, Althusser belonged to a family that had been deported to Algeria in the late nineteenth century. Derrida and Cixous, though French, were part of the ousted populace of Spain whose ancestors were evicted along with the Moors and whose confiscated family fortunes were spent by Spanish royalty in sponsoring and financing early expeditions, such as those of Christopher Columbus, to Latin America. Memmi and Fanon, early exponents of postcolonialism, were also linked to the Maghreb: Memmi was born in Tunis while Fanon went on to join the revolution there. Fanon's famous works, *The Wretched of the Earth* and *Black Skin, White Masks*, which are seminal to the rise of postcolonialism as a discipline, emerged from his involvement in the Algerian struggle for liberation. Likewise, Lyotard and Bourdieu had links with Algeria, whether in terms of joining the revolution or in carrying out research (Young 2001: 414).[21] Young even alludes to the poststructuralism of these theoreticians as 'Franco-Maghrebian theory' because 'its theoretical interventions have been actively concerned with the task of undoing the ideological heritage of French colonialism and with rethinking the premises, assumptions and protocols of its centrist, imperial culture' (Young 2001: 414). All these theorists were 'othered' from dominant French culture even though they become part of mainstream French theory many years later. Suffice it to say, for Young, poststructuralism arises out of colonialism, its western linkages notwithstanding.[22] Structuralism originated in Prague as a defence against imperialist thought just as poststructuralism developed in Algeria and the Maghreb as an anti-western line of attack. Historically, too, postcolonialism can be linked to post-structuralism and its critique of the project of humanism owing to the anti-eurocentric beginnings and the revisionary strategies inherent in both. Even if postcolonialism is believed to emanate from western academia, and thus to be hegemonic, its ventures go well beyond 'western' poststructuralist theories because it enters the 'colonial space' and retains the 'colonial other' as its central concern (Gikandi 2004: 116–17). By this logic, however, even Bhabha's radical chic, which has received so much flak, can be recommended for extending Derrida's notion of 'difference' to the 'history of the colonial moment' (Bhabha 1994: 32). Postcolonial theory enunciates the notion of cultural difference precisely at the moment that poststructuralism critically examines western humanism and the Enlightenment tradition. But postcolonial theory does not linger long enough to consider the nation or the nation's people as it strides on to deconstruct what remains the only ostensible sign of the sovereignty of the people.

To counter the other objection, that postcolonial theorists have betrayed the 'real' sites of resistance and political protest as a result of migration to the west, Young writes spiritedly: 'Now-a-days, no one really knows where an author "is" when they read a book, apart from guarded information about institutional affiliations on the dust-jacket, and nor should it matter' (Young 2001: 62). He makes no distinction between academics living in the west, those looking westward in spite of living in their own societies, and those who spend a good deal of their time researching in the west even though they consider themselves to 'belong' to the third world, since all of them are involved in revisiting hegemonies in order to unravel history and write it anew, especially if globalization is believed to be an extension of imperialism (Young 2001: 62). As far as the migrant community is concerned, they hardly belong to the class of jet-setting individuals Ahmad and Dirlik have in mind; such people, on the contrary, try hard not to break ties with the culture they have left behind. Some of these people attend educational institutions in the west and maintain their own forms of protest in the face of racism and the everyday struggles of their existence in an alien country. The long oppressed, on reaching the unfamiliar location of their new homes, voice political concerns that are strongly underpinned by their personal suffering. For them, postcolonial studies is not some kind of hegemonic discipline that emerged from western universities but a consequence of tensions between the settlers and the populations of the west (Young 2001: 62). It can also be argued that postcolonial studies grew simultaneously with the ongoing criticism of traditional western writing which was developed by intellectuals and academics outside the postcolonial world. This must be among the few instances where the west articulated a resistance against its own policies relating to the major parts of the world it had once controlled.[23] It would be pertinent to note, however, that Ahmad and Dirlik target those third-world intellectuals like Bhabha and Spivak who hardly belong with the suffering migratory communities who pointedly carried with them the pain and struggle of their sites of origin.[24] Criticism of postcolonial studies for its opportunism is unreasonable to the extent of failing to recognize the links between an enduring tradition of liberatory writing (predating Bhabha and Spivak by decades) and decolonization movements, not to speak of those prophets of 'postcolonialism' such as Fanon, Cabral, Césaire, Gandhi, Kenyatta, Nyerere, Nkrumah and Senghor who laid the groundwork for later critics. Even as the critics deplore its excessive reliance on 'post-ist' methodology as a sign of its continued acceptance of western hegemony, postcolonial practice is an ongoing process in cultures outside the west, in many guises and under various names.[25]

To be fair to contemporary theorists like Spivak, it could be argued that her project is one of interrogating the elite interpreter. The reason why she insists that subaltern identity cannot be recovered has to do as much with the critic's own elite placement as an interventionist as with the inadequacy of working nativism as an alternative (Spivak 1984, 1988a, 1988b). In 'The Rani of Sirmur', one of her essays on *sati* or sanctioned suicide, Spivak does attempt to open up a space for the Rani in the process of interrogating her own position as an investigator. The Rani's narrative of emergence can lie only within the archive installed by the Company officials, for in the act of *sati*, she is constituted between 'patriarchal subject-formation and imperialist object-constitution' (Spivak 1984: 144). As Spivak writes, 'Within the two contending versions of freedom, the constitution of the female subject *in life* was thoroughly undermined' (Spivak 1984: 145). Spivak's error lies in neglecting the site of protest in her effort to warn against the dangers of partial representation. Her detractors' error, on the other hand, is that of interpreting postcolonial criticism only from the limited perspectives of Bhabha and Spivak, concluding that postcolonial studies does not engage with praxis.[26]

The employment of a poststructuralist methodology as a handy tool to critique the grand narrative of the nation, the over-reliance on Anderson's concept of imagined communities in relation to the growing global diaspora that seems to provide fertile ground for the hybrid articulations of postcolonial studies, and the consequent flexibility of boundaries that creates hostility to the nation as a potent form of individual and group identity – all these need to be examined if postcolonial studies is to become more than simply a cultural monitor of migrancy and capital flows, just as Marxist theory needs to become more 'internationalist' if postcolonial studies is to find common ground with it.[27] In their articulation of the nation as a cultural construct rooted more in symbolic than historical-material factors, postcolonial theorists fail to see that culturally reified sentiments within the nation are challenged by the processes of modernization and social reform. It is at such moments that cultural nationalism shows its regressive aspects. The requirements of a modern state and the aspirations of the masses are hardly compatible with a nostalgic retreat into culture. Cultural abstractions underpinning nationalist representations, alone, cannot be considered responsible for the rise of anti-colonial nations.[28] However, when Marxists criticize postcolonial theory as elitist and self-indulgent, they neglect to examine their own inadequacies, such as their inability to see nation-states as instruments facilitating the establishment of foreign investments instead of playing a supervisory or mediatory role. It is important also not to over-privilege the nation-state given its ineffectiveness in removing inequalities and asymmetries among men and women or privileged and underprivileged sections of its people.[29] Not only do these failings raise questions about the nature of the liberty and freedom of the nation following independence struggles, they also strengthen the ongoing critique of binarism on which dependency theories base themselves, and which continue to be the benchmark for the Marxist interpretation of oppression at the point of production. These debates foreground the differences between the nation and the nation-state, the former a cultural category, the focus of postcolonial analysis, whereas the latter is a material concept that Marxists find useful in explaining the regulating of capitalist production, both of which have to be brought to a crisis.

Apart from relating academic criticism to political praxis and developing its roots in political activism, postcolonial studies will have to sort out the politics of location if the concept of the nation is to have any worth. If contemporary postcolonial studies is to be linked with its celebrated ancestors, it must be remembered that the deeply political nature of the movements of decolonization that gave rise to their liberatory writings focused primarily on the nation as the major living political reality. The many examples of the cooperation, bloodshed and sacrifice involved in the formation of postcolonial nations are instances of the 'imagined community' intersecting with real time. The glorification of the peasantry is an appropriation by the nationalist intelligentsia of a site of national identity which is related to territory or land that is part of the nation's past and remains untouched by the culture of imperialism. By escaping modernity and Enlightenment, the peasantry survive outside discourse-making, thereby becoming identified with unadulterated and pristine reality. Curiously, poststructuralists themselves appropriate this very field of the uncorrupted but voiceless native in their anti-humanist ideology. In fact, orientalists, nationalists, Marxists and subalternists, have all, in their own celebratory or disingenuous ways, used the sub-proletariat in their works. To make postcolonial studies part of 'nationalitarian politics', in Lazarus's formulation (1997: 45), is unavoidable, since the nation is the only site which can yoke together the local and the global.[30] If postcolonial studies is to be relevant today, it must become the voice of the people and theorize about movements against globalization, rather than becoming part of its grand design.

III

Although the terms – postcolonialism, postcolonial theory and postcolonial studies – have been used assiduously throughout the discussion so far, and have been briefly explained earlier, we need to arrive at a more careful understanding of all three so that they are not used randomly or as substitutes for one another. 'Postcolonialism', it should be clear by this point, represents a philosophy, rather than just an academic discipline, that seeks to encourage radical politics and engagement with popular struggles, which includes the study of the history of colonialism as a reminder of anti-imperialist politics.[31] 'Postcolonial theory', on the other hand, has its own baggage and tends to be related to western theories and is thus termed elitist by many people in academia. Having said that, it is not as though theory has no application to issues relating to almost every aspect of postcolonialism such as gender, race, migrancy, diaspora, nation, English studies, and so on. Finally, 'postcolonial studies' is the discipline that has still not embraced many of the economic and political issues relating to postcolonialism largely because it is taught in the English departments of universities where an emphasis on cultural studies is predominant (Loomba 1998b: 40). As a discipline it includes the study of postcolonial theory and postcolonial literature.

As has been argued, it is postcolonial studies that is often accused of failing to make an intervention in the real politics of the people as a result of its academic methodologies focused on modes of textual interpretation. The discipline is undoubtedly derived from movements against colonialism, yet its relationship with poststructuralism and postmodernism is most often used to highlight its apolitical nature. Postcolonial studies is thus faulted for being excessively textual and 'thin'. Not only should postcolonial studies not disregard third-world national liberation movements, it should also depend more judiciously on western theory so that its excessive reliance on simulacra and anti-essentialism can be kept at bay. It is worth asking the question why the classroom cannot establish a connection with the real histories of the people or why university teaching does not breed the kind of responsible intellectual of which Edward Said spoke. Why do we have to deal with 'so-called' reality in literary studies today? Clearly, this has to do with the abiding link between postcolonialism and anti-foundationalism, a link postcolonial theory has done much to promote. If postcolonial studies were released from 'theory', we might still have postcolonial moments capable of establishing a correspondence with the world outside. In order to become interventionist, postcolonial studies per se does not need to become politically active; on the contrary, it should shed its 'thin' textualism in favour of 'a richer critical and historical analysis' (Loomba 1998b: 42) that would include questions of identity, struggle and change intermixed with the politics of our times. An important part of such an academic study would be its relatedness with political activity in the sense of becoming a medium that supports and disseminates marginalized voices and resistance movements across the world, so that subordination to the growing power of the west might be diminished. Only then might a meaningful relationship exist between subjecthood and the dominating market forces of globalization, or between agency and the ambiguities of nationalist thought.

From this point of view, Shahid Amin's *Event, Metaphor, Memory* – which recounts the history of the 'rioting' in 1922 in which 23 policemen were burnt to death, prompting Gandhi to call off the Non-cooperation movement against the British in India – would be a suitable example of the kind of writing that can be included within postcolonial studies (Amin 1996). So would Vandana Shiva's *Staying Alive*, which documents with intensity women's roles both in challenging the universalist claims of patriarchy with examples of diversity as well as in opposing the concept of power as violence with the alternative concept of non-violence as power (Shiva 1989). I use the word 'postcolonial' and 'postcolonialism' pretty much in this sense. In Chapter 4, however, where I focus more closely on 'postcolonial studies', I refer mainly to that postcolonial theory and criticism which is part of university curricula in the United States. While the distinctions between the terminology should be carefully maintained, such hair-splitting concerning the many forms and usages of the 'postcolonial' perhaps only reduces the powerful charge that was generated by its historical and political origins and makes one look repeatedly over one's shoulder. But so long as we are able to convey that charge, the bifurcation of postcolonialism into its linguistic variations to convey its separate aspects may not always be necessary.

This book seeks to determine the relationships between the politics of postcolonialism, nationalism and globalization, and to confront the new imperialism of the United States in view of its institutionalization of postcolonial studies. The following chapter considers how national sovereignty is nullified in the context of the neoimperialism of the global market. I explore the 'mythical' ways in which postcolonial studies has represented the nation and, in doing so, obscured the political action and resistance strategies of native cultures who have needed to stand up to the authority of the nation-state as much as to the eurocentric powers outside it. The recurring motif that binds the project together is the predicament of subcultures in the developing world as they struggle to escape the subordinate position in which the centre would like them to stay. In its critical approach, postcolonial studies has failed to show up how the formation of the nation-state has been deeply imbricated in capital formation, stifling insurgent socialisms in the course of its global progress. Obviously, neither a wholly 'materialist' nor an entirely 'culturalist' analysis can give us an adequate understanding of the nation-state.

Chapter 3 relates postcolonialism to globalization processes. I point out how postcolonial analyses have grown simultaneously with the increase of global capital and have even become complicit with it, particularly in the new millennium marked by increasing US intervention. These are unresolved problems, and what we need is a better understanding of the issues confronting the former colonial countries in a post/neocolonial world, especially in view of the worldwide surge of protest and resistance. Contemporary global relations between north and south cannot be resolved by altogether neglecting the binary logic of core and periphery since civil insurgencies and political protests strongly reassert the existence of embedded power structures of the world. In Chapter 4, I observe how capital has moved from the traditional colonial space to the only remaining superpower that, apparently without guilt, has enthusiastically jumped on the postcolonial bandwagon. An examination of US culture through the prism of postcolonial thought jostles with our understandings of race, ethnicity and migration which have set the parameters of American Studies for many years. More significantly, the idea of US 'exceptionalism', and the recent resurgence of its aggressive nationhood, intrude upon the definitions of postcolonialism that will be established in the course of what follows.

2

THE END OF THE NATION?

I

As decolonization struggles began with the culmination of the Second World War, postcolonial nations revelled in the end of European subjugation. Today, however, especially in the contemporary debates on liberalization, it is clear that none of these new states are inclined to be left out of the 'rapidly shrinking global village' (Phalkey 1999: 38). What we are now confronting is a transitional nation-state, one in which the desire to hold on to traditional lifestyles and customs struggles against the urge to join the 'new world order' or the era of globalization. As the erstwhile empire of the west endeavours to come to terms with new political possibilities after long-drawn-out liberation struggles involving the subversion of inherited language structures and the reassertion of native ethnic values, we paradoxically witness the obsessive determination of former colonies to participate in the mechanisms of a 'global cultural economy' (Appadurai 2000: 1806). The nation-state, for instance, is marked by both the politics of resistance to neoimperialism with talk of 'unity and integrity' (in India, for example) and submission to the world economy in the name of development. For this reason, many have argued that the former colonies end up complying with global networks of trade and the present economic hegemony, thereby disowning the hard-won fruits of national struggles.[1]

The meaning and character of the nation-state has changed enormously in the context of the global economy. Global pressures have exacerbated the insecurities of third-world states owing to the compelling nature of market forces. It seems that nation-states have virtually played into the hands of superpowers and have retained little control over their own economic choices. The nation-state may be just as necessary now as it was in the days of the earlier decolonization struggles, but its interaction with the forces of globalization has permitted a post-national thinking beyond centre-periphery models into a heretofore uncharted space without peoples, without 'local' culture, without even the conflicting claims of homeland and diaspora. The response of formerly colonized societies to the political and cultural authority of Europe, and now of the US, may no longer be seen within the binary opposition of master and slave, but rather as an ambiguous terrain marked by the recovery and resilience of indigenous societies that has changed the complexion of the nation-state.

While the present chapter heading refers only to the 'nation', an interrogation of the future of the nation-*state* as a consequence of globalization will be as much of a concern in the discussion to follow. From the viewpoint of postcolonial studies, both the nation and the nation-state are to be dismissed: where the one is a cultural imaginary, the other is in a state of obsolescence with the surge of global capitalism in the world. My use of 'nation' and 'nation-state' is concomitant with their imagined and real status; it is more or less customary now to take the former as a cultural construction and the latter as a political entity. (Having explained their usage, I shall not use quotation marks any longer when referring to the former.) However, there is another dimension to this discussion that is significant. Even though it is said that the nation-state is spent, the resurgence of the nation, time and again, despite dislocation and the movement of capital, is a force to be reckoned with. In such times, it is the nation-state that is weak but not the nation. In this situation, the possibility of resuscitating 'pure' national cultures within circumstances that evoke the binaries of the oppressor and the oppressed may be very strong. Thus the nation becomes as real as it is imaginary in postcolonial discourse. However, while nation-states continue to exist, the nation – real or imagined – is effectually lost.

What is relevant here is an investigation of the intrinsic changes in both nationalistic tendencies as well as western intervention after decolonization. By exploring the nature of the environment of market capitalism, I will evaluate, first, the ambivalences of national sovereignty: the fact that states today open themselves up to foreign investments while also clinging to the rhetoric of nativism and authenticity. A reflection on the possible meanings and implications of decolonization allows us to consider whether the 'freedom' of ex-colonized cultures is anything other than rhetorical and whether the different agendas of the 'victor' and the 'vanquished' are at all clear-cut and demarcated. Secondly, I focus on locating the liberatory potential inherent in postcolonial studies. Do postcolonial approaches struggle against the tide and suggest a reclamation of the nation, or do they merely swim with the capital flows? Can the nation retain its political identity in spite of that disdain of nationalist constructions which is a feature of postcolonial studies? The tragedy of the nation has always been its vexed nature: nationalism continues to be an important factor in national identity even as the concept has changed over the last few decades. Although the idea of anti-colonial nationalism implies moving away from western economic practices that undercut the very concept of freedom, the nation, as it stands, is equally committed to a modernity which introduces market capitalism. Owing to enormous capital inflows and increased migration, a global-imaginary has replaced a national-imaginary (Szeman 2003: 28) based on the logic of the implacable nature of globalization. The history of globalization in the west and its effects on the nation-states of the decolonized world will be traced at the outset, leading finally to an assessment of Hardt and Negri's *Empire* as a prelude to evaluating the contemporary relevance of the state in a globalized climate.

I want to begin by asking the most pertinent question: is this the end of the nation-state? An emerging nation-state has a peculiar history. After attaining independence, all the symbols of autonomy are at once thrust upon it. In many ways, it may well have jumped out of the frying pan into the fire. The new nation-state begins to parade its national flag and anthem, its own currency, its place on the world map. Every year, it celebrates its independence day with great fanfare and solemnity through parades and exhibitions.[2] These are marks of its identity, an identity that cannot (or should not) be defined against its Other, the former colonialist. On the one hand, the emphasis on a collective native identity may become a point of departure for many nation-states, but in the presence of different core groups, religious practices, sects, cults, and so on, a nativist alternative will, at best, be partial and prejudiced, being only a small part of the national dilemma of resolving its 'identity crisis'. On the other hand, if the notion of a monolithic homogeneous identity were dismantled in order to develop an alternative perspective on self-representative accounts, various communities and segmented identities distinguished by language, caste, occupation and geographical location would stand diminished, and the new nation-state would be thus jeopardized. Partha Chatterjee offers a different perspective on the resolution of the problem of the nation-state. He explains how states claim sovereignty on the basis of native identities (home, women, culture) yet imitate or borrow ceaselessly from the material world (identified with the colonizer) because of the pressure of keeping up with the rest of the globe. Important as such borrowings are for the new nation-states, they constantly struggle to maintain a balance between the 'home' and the 'world' with the aim of perpetuating the discourse of progress in much the same way as did the industrialized countries before them (Chatterjee 1993a: 6). While on that course, they also try to maintain their economic dignity without excessive dependence on any western power.

Nation-states persisted until the end of the Cold War long after decolonization struggles were over. Between the beginning of the Cold War and the end of the 1980s, they played one superpower off against another. The superpowers, for their part, refrained from asserting direct political control because of the anxiety of losing their allies to the other superpower (Johnson 2004: 258). At this time, most decolonized countries believed they had the freedom to plan their development in ways compatible with their own economic and cultural traditions. Although they did not have a surfeit of industry and technology, they were able to rely greatly on the export of agricultural produce to the rich nations of the north and sought the means of industrialization in exchange. But by the 1980s, exhaustion had crept into both the US and the

USSR. Soon, with the economic collapse of the USSR, only one superpower remained – the United States (aided by its primary partner, Britain) – which set itself up as the major power in the world. In the aftermath of the Second World War, the US had already put in place the Marshall Plan, through which economic relationships were built with European and Japanese partners. This was one of the earliest efforts at invoking postwar global ties. Many of these alliances were anti-Communist in ideology. Even before the collapse of the Soviet bloc, US-backed institutions such as the World Bank and the International Monetary Fund had been employed to assist old nation-states towards economic development through the temptations of free trade, unhindered investment and the promise of a quick entry into the new world order.

The new initiatives taken by the US – including the jettisoning of fixed exchange rates based on the gold standard and the disposal of almost all regulatory controls following the fiscal policies of US presidents, particularly those advanced by Richard Nixon who practically traduced the doctrine of Keynesianism – more or less discounted government intervention in the maintenance of a sound economy. Henceforth, the 'free market' became the 'new religion' by means of which virtually all government attempts to safeguard the economy, except for regulating inflation through the supply of money and credit, were removed (Aronowitz 2003: 185). The rise of conservative governments under Ronald Reagan in the United States and Margaret Thatcher in Britain saw the revival of international trade, foreign investment and privatization and an enthusiasm for the development of the 'global village', signifying 'neoliberalism', which presaged the beginning of the decline of nation-states. This was also known as the 'Washington consensus' in politics, 'neoclassical economics' among academics, and 'globalism' or 'globalization' in the world at large (Johnson 2004: 260). Thatcher and Reagan together manoeuvred what David Harvey calls a process of 'accumulation by dispossession' (Harvey 2003: 137). As a result, Britain in the 1980s witnessed a rapid privatization of housing, water, electricity, telecommunications, energy, transportation and other public concerns initiated by a leader who was, ironically, the elected representative of the people.

Capitalism secured its eventual victory with the end of the Cold War. A state of war is known to keep alive the fervour of patriotism. The end of the Cold War duly reduced nationalist sentiment and ignited the spark of a new transnational capitalist mode of production giving way to the 'new world order'. The liberal prognosis concerning the end of history appeared to have come into its own:

> It seemed, for a brief moment, that Lenin was wrong and that Kautsky might be right – an ultra-imperialism based on a 'peaceful' collaboration between all the major capitalist powers (now symbolized by the grouping known as the G7, expanded to the G8 to incorporate Russia, albeit under the hegemony of US leadership) was possible – and that the cosmopolitan character of finance capital (symbolized by the meetings of the World Economic Forum in Davos) would be its founding ideology. (Harvey 2003: 68–9)

The suspension of class struggle, so important for national cohesion, and the investment of foreign capital are now major features of the new world order. Economic activity on such a global scale has radically weakened the power of labour, which was one of the reasons for 'the decline of the nation-state as the core of political sovereignty and the mediator of economic and political protest' (Aronowitz 2003: 186). The new politico-economic situation is now able to dispense with labour unions once so integral to the nation-state.[3] As less and less labour is required in the processes of production, the nation-state undergoes the shift from an industrial to an informational economy. Although labour unions are not altogether unimportant in terms of public services, they are hardly likely to be considered integral to any collective resistance movement which might arise among workers owing to the existence of transnational enterprises. The rapidly growing transnational corporations characteristically unmoor themselves from centre-periphery binaries as well as from the limits of a national territory or identity, crossing boundaries with the sole aim of increasing profits.[4] What the *Communist Manifesto* claimed about the spread of capitalism more than a hundred years ago is just as relevant today: 'The need of a constantly expanding market for its products chases the bourgeoisie over the whole surface of the globe. It must nestle everywhere, settle everywhere, establish connections everywhere ... it creates a world after its own image' (Marx and Engels 1967: 223–4). This stage of capitalism, when 'the Third World move[s] from an affiliation with the second world to the first' (Young 1998: 6), marks perhaps the first stirrings of postcolonial studies with its accompanying critique of the nation.

The immediate reaction of developing nation-states to the onslaught of transnational corporations (TNCs) lay in setting up organizations for mutual aid and reciprocity. As such, we have the SAARC (South Asian Association for Regional Cooperation, 1985), OPEC (Organization of Petroleum Exporting Countries, 1960), the non-aligned movement (1950s) and the Bandung Conference (1955).[5] Notwithstanding these efforts, border crossings into new territories to maximize economic advantage continue to be randomly pursued by the TNCs. What facilitates this process of infiltration is the inchoate nature and namelessness of the class of people who make up the TNCs. Their products are sold without any reference to their source countries since only brand names matter in the market (Miyoshi 2000: 1877). Being neither place-bound nor constrained by national passion, this class of people are truly decentralized, moved only by the logic of the conglomerate. National labels become a thing of the past as corporations and companies move in to acquire control of nation-states. For the erstwhile colonies, the new masters are now the markets (Strange 2004: 220). The TNC workforce owes its loyalty more to the corporation than to its country of origin. Since TNCs are blatantly self-serving and profit-centric, they are not too concerned about the welfare of their labour force. The state, for its part, cannot take up welfare programmes for the labour force since responsibility for the people has in many cases been turned over to the TNCs. The power of the local, underpinned by culture-specific identities, becomes diffused and decentred as the new global society is fashioned through a plethora of treaties and networks. The diminishing role of labour and of material modes of production are affected also by a growing market obsession with the spectre of 'futures': stakes are made in terms of prospective deals as investors gauge the stock market indices and future interest rates in an attempt to make money in the present (Adam 2002: 22). The markets also, in turn, encroach upon future natural resources such as fossil fuel and harness them in the present. In this scenario, TNCs can even prosecute national governments if they fail to open their doors to imports since 'sovereignty can be inconvenient' (Galeano 1997: 208). The strength of corporations compared to most nation-states is indeed enormous:

> The emerging global order is spearheaded by a few hundred corporate giants, many of them bigger than most sovereign nations. Ford's economy is larger than Saudi Arabia's and Norway's. Philip Morris's annual sales exceed New Zealand's gross domestic product. The multinational corporation of twenty years ago carried on separate operations in many different countries and tailored its operations to local conditions. In the 1990s large business enterprises, [and] even some smaller ones, have the technological means and strategic vision to burst old limits – of time, space, national boundaries, language, custom and ideology. (Barnet and Cavanagh 1994: 14)

Considering that transnational corporations have larger investments and greater capital liquidity than many nation-states can command, it is no wonder that sweeping claims about the demise of those states are being made.[6]

Globalized capitalism has re-fashioned the pattern of almost all nation-states in the world so that the 'new world order', as George W. Bush would have it, is borderless (Ohmae 2004: 214). The network of production has expanded to such an extent that it is no longer possible to say that the performance of IBM in India is a sign of the technological well-being of the US. We have to rethink why we regard economic progress in the west as a sign of their nationalism. The information-hungry new generation that has undergone the 'California-ization' of taste (Ohmae 2004: 217) – such that they have much more in common with their Nike-flaunting, Levi-sporting mates elsewhere in the world than with the older generation in their own countries – have created their own nation-space by appropriating a slice of the global economy. The exclusivity of nation-states and the traces of local, indigenous cultures are now being steadily consumed by the sweeping anonymity of the TNCs and the culture of shopping malls and multiplex cinemas, thereby reducing national history and culture to '[mere] variants of one "universal"'(Miyoshi 2000: 1882).[7] There is no resolution to the problem of attaining an equilibrium between 'home' and the 'world' any longer. It is thus that nation-states have become borderless. The orthodox nation-state, as the nationalist generation views it, appears to be a sort of dinosaur that has not been able to adapt to globalized conditions (Garrett 2004: 233).

As nation-states are reduced to being no more than market units, the question of territory, so important to its earlier conception, loses much of its national character owing to the ideological disconnection with 'homeland' or 'motherland'. This is not to say that territory is no longer held sacred; the nation-state still protects its territory zealously, but its very 'transnational' character, in that capital is no longer confined to any particular territory, results in the ideological dematerialization of land. Although a growth in economic activity appears to be of great advantage for states enabling them to purchase cheaper higher quality products, it cannot be denied that the ideological disappearance of borders and boundaries in this 'manufactured jungle' (Bauman 1998: 60) is linked with their growing decline.

Global capitalism thus becomes the new name of colonialism. The primary aspiration of new states – to ensure the greatest good of the greatest number – is lost in the wave of global give and take and the opening up of national boundaries. The ensuing contradiction between localism and third-world ventures into global capital shows up as problematic, since the 'global' now includes 'transnational movements and influences' within national boundaries whereas the 'local' contains corruptions of the so-called quintessentially indigenous identity (John 1999: 198–9). The two terms still retain their old meanings and yet get mixed up with the kind of politics for which we do not, as yet, have a nomenclature. After many decades, the Indian economy, for example, has begun to look outward towards the world. However, this is happening at a time when the right-wing ideology of Hindutva (the aggressive idea of Hindu nationhood) is becoming significantly powerful, integrating forces of fascism within the nation-state as much as outside it.[8] We are witnessing both strong assertions of nativism and an utter reliance on international technology. Voices proclaiming 'little' nationalisms are growing louder in these rapidly 'developing' societies as a self-styled nationalist bourgeoisie is on the rise. This class of people have contradictory interests: they want to boost the inflow of capital by encouraging liberalization but also protect their ideological cultural constructs. They obstruct any radical politics but profess loyalty to tradition and roots by 'propagating the discourse of Authenticity and cultural differentialism in the name of Islam in one space, Hinduism in another, in order to forge protofascist nationalisms' (Ahmad 1995a: 12).[9]

The unfortunate consequence of such nationalism is likely to be in the direction of integrating jingoist identities that are barely able to check the march of globalization. A case in point is the BJP, the second largest political party in India, currently forming the opposition; while not isolationalist in its policies it nevertheless fans Hindu passion nationwide. During its tenure in government (1998–2004), it was not averse to foreign collaborations with TNCs on infra-structure projects related to power, roads, telecommunications, chemicals and other industries, but it rallied against the setting up of the Enron thermal plant, during the Congress regime, on grounds of ideological purity.[10] From this view, huddling uneasily under the rubric of a rabid right-wing ideology would not augur well for the complex ways and means by which historical circumstances are generated for national integration. The coexistence of the idea of the larger nation-state existing for the general good and the multifarious local nationalisms garnered by national bourgeoisies – the one mindlessly ushering in global investment and the other resisting it (or so we think) – creates a complexity in the nation-state form which is difficult to comprehend within a socialist framework. These complex processes working on a multiplicity of sites can be taken as postcolonial moments that have to be rescued in order to understand both the larger nation-state that regulates the inflow of capital and the little nation that stirs up fascism while promoting a certain localism.

Despite the contradictory claims of the nation-state in both its local and global manifestations, the culture of corporatism and the transition to a capitalist economy are ushered in by the state itself in the name of progress and beneficence for all.[11] The goals of initiating education, health schemes, welfare for people, old age pensions and the removal of poverty all appear to be within reach so long as the nation-state pursues the trajectory of globalization. But along with proclamations that a globalized state will initiate a democratic utopia in which all citizens will be equal before law and elect their representatives, the entire enterprise of securing the conditions of capital accumulation, of privatization, the imposition of intellectual property rights, the very 'sale' of nature itself – rivers and land – for investment is regulated by the state.[12] The principles of commonality and diffusion underlying the 'global' seems to imply that there will be no antagonistic parties or groups in the one homogeneous global environment. But the word 'global' is a misnomer: in real terms, both these principles efface the very possibility of protest and resistance. Alliances between nation-states and globalization are worked out in terms of ensuring a greater flow of exchange across boundaries, which suggests the disappearance of the oppressor and the oppressed, and along with that, of the very sites of resistance. 'Global', thus far, has never meant 'everywhere' or 'everybody', since globalization chooses its localities carefully in order to maximize profits, working on the principle of 'maximum exclusion' (Miyoshi 1997: 55).[13] While borders have ceased to matter, fences are erected against one's own people. This is the paradox of the nation-state which has to be understood in all its contradictory potential: it is collaborative with the world market system rather than with its own local economies, becoming an 'ambivalent player' (Rai 1999: 27) that fails to defend its own marginalized peoples as it sets up shop in the corporate world. It is in this very contrariness, sometimes, that the continued significance of the nation-state lies, albeit in its many regressive forms and ideologies.

Even classic colonialism was no less culpable of reaping the benefits of commerce through alliances with a comprador class. The East India Company and the United Fruit Company in Latin America are examples, and in both cases the common people bore the brunt of their activities. Even though increased investment raises GNP in a developing country, that can never be a determinant for an actual and balanced increase in the standard of living. Globalization is as much a discourse about equity as nationalism and the nation-state, and likewise one in which the playing field is certainly not level, despite Friedman's insistence (2005: 5). When national leaders celebrate greater democracy and homogeneity of classes in hypocritical self-congratulatory speeches, it is usually a camouflage for even wider disparities. 'Main Street', in Žižek's words, 'depends on a thriving Wall Street'. Such is the disparity between the two that 'self-propelling and self-augmenting financial circulation is its only dimension of the Real, in contrast to the reality of production' (Žižek 2009: 13, 14). The various kinds of resistance to oppression enumerated in the next chapter testify to the inequality globalization has brought in its wake.

In many third-world countries, the employment of bioeconomics and biopolitics have facilitated the spread of agribusinesses into what was traditional small-scale farming, while the forays of science and technology into what were hitherto labour-intensive production processes have severely curtailed the role of nation-states in governance (Aronowitz 2003: 186–7). China, while still officially a Communist state of long-standing, has privatized monumentally, giving up social welfare and pension schemes. Although it has quickly become the supreme economic power in Asia, this has been at the cost of withdrawing protections and curtailing social spending at the behest of the state. Chinese farmers dependent on family farms are slowly being absorbed by urbanization in order to recover from the take-over by agribusinesses. The introduction of a free market economy has reversed the achievements of decades of class struggle, an important component of state power. Whereas earlier the states that formed the coalition of non-aligned countries encouraged resistance through the power of unions against the tactical interests of the western alliance, these residual nation-states, for all the nostalgia attached to them, now no longer hold out the promise of welfare and equality for all. Their system of taxation, for instance, is partisan and lop-sided, benefiting some sections at the cost of others. If protectionist policies, though a short-term measure, are advantageous for industry, they can be a handicap for consumers who may find trade desirable owing to the competitiveness of the market.

If they are to continue with the principles enshrined in national ideologies at the time of gaining independence, the postcolonial states will have to set up barriers to foreign trade and investment and thus decrease the gap between the owners of capital and the workers. This will require labour-intensive industry where outsourcing will have to be gradually diminished. Whenever trade weakens the standards of domestic practices, it can hardly be called fair, especially when it is accompanied by the absence of social insurance. Increased trade ties, however, weaken the concept of the welfare state even in the west, a concept which the left had spent much effort establishing in the 40 years following the Depression. To maintain social democracy, liberalization cannot be embraced freely, although opponents of social democracy would argue that too much public spending by government is also unproductive: social security, pensions, unemployment benefits, care for the sick and the old are never good for growth. Where does this contemporary contrariness of the nation-state place postcolonial studies, a discipline that was meant to be an anti-eurocentric defence against all kinds of imperial control?

II

Having looked at the rise of globalization and its effects on the dynamics of the nation-state, we can now lock horns with postcolonial studies, which appears not to have represented the nation-state in ways that might exploit its emancipatory possibilities. There are several reasons for this. First, the discipline has fixated itself to such an extent on what we understand as 'discourse' that, for it, the real world outside discourse now all but ceases to exist. Indeed, 'real' can be mentioned only within quotation marks or prefixed by the phrase 'so-called' in the works of most postcolonial theorists: we belong to 'so-called' nations; we espouse a 'so-called' nationalism. In postcolonial writing, the nation-state is differentiated from the nation precisely when one wants to distinguish the real from the mythical, a differentiation which will be observed while employing the term 'nation' in this section. From Anderson to Gilroy and Bhabha, several critics of the 1980s and 1990s tend to be wary of nations and nationalisms. Secondly, the turn in postcolonial studies towards multiculturalism, migration and diaspora coincides with the growth of global capital as labour has migrated westward. As capital and labour both travel further afield, the nation-state is bound to lose its 'ties of territoriality' (Davis 1978: 6) and become diffused and decentred, both for its diasporic population and for those who remain within its boundaries. It is for this reason that Anderson's concept of 'imagined communities' (see Anderson 1983) lends itself conveniently to a linguistic workout: sometimes appearing as 'diasporic imaginary' (Mishra 1996: 21), at other times as 'nation space' (Bhabha 1990b: 299).[14] As analysed in the previous chapter, it is the diasporic community of academics who have largely emerged as forerunners in the exercise of redefining national frontiers in terms utterly disconnected with the real. In interpreting the nation as a discursive construction, the contribution of postmodernism cannot be overestimated.

Three preoccupations of postcolonial studies with regard to the concept of nation are perhaps responsible for the criticisms accorded to it: the emphasis on the cultural aspect of nationalism which does much to damage its political stability; the insistence that the nation neglects its lower orders, especially after the achievement of independence; and finally, the view that nationalism is a derivative of western ideologies, a criticism that discounts the very conception of political praxis on the part of native societies and their ability to evolve their own philosophies of governance (Chrisman 2004:

185).[15] Anderson's *Imagined Communities* (1983) and Chatterjee's *The Nation and its Fragments* (1993a) contributed a great deal to the understanding of nationalism as a construction of cultural categories. Both Anderson and Chatterjee argue that nationalism harks back to antiquity as much as it covets western materialism in order to embrace modernity. A range of diverse theorists of nationalism speak about the nation's culturalist reliance on folk traditions, religion, rural dialects, village communities – in short, on pastness – to underscore cultural uniqueness and kindle national consciousness.[16] But one may not be too easily persuaded by their arguments. Arguably, the nation's material concerns may be distinguished from the cultural, since its chief motivation is 'mobilization' and 'self-determination' and not the reification of cultural identities (Chrisman 2004: 186). The modern state has not been realized by retreating into a homogenous notion of culture or even by reconnecting with fixed roots and cultural codes which have been only partially instrumental in bringing about a revolution in the circumstances of the colonized. For the establishment of an independent nation following an anti-colonial struggle, a culturally imagined unification can, at best, only be an accompaniment to a mass political movement. Nationalists like Cabral and Fanon articulated national resistance through heterogeneous mixtures of the precolonial and the modern, in combinations that did not rely on any formulaic division between the two. A closer look 'at political and economic sovereignty over a finite landmass', which would involve a sense of physical possession over material resources rather than a reliance on cultural consciousness, is the way to bring back the decolonized nation into these debates (Chrisman 2004: 186, 187).

All the same, a materialist rather than a culturalist view itself tends to overlook the basic inadequacies of nation-states-to-be under colonial domination. Budding nations are scarcely in a position to implement decisions regarding territory, trade, governance or citizenry, elements paramount to their consciousness as a nation but as yet not within their grasp. The only manner of overcoming these shortfalls is to accentuate the nation's precolonial cultural 'authenticity', as outlined by Anderson,

Chatterjee and others. How else, as Said would say, 'does a culture seeking to become independent of imperialism imagine its own past?' (Said 1993: 258). Nationalism could not be successfully achieved without creating the divide between the spiritual 'east' and the material 'west' engineered by the indigenous elite. In spite of imitating continually on the plane of materiality, it is on the level of spirituality that the nation is deemed 'sovereign' even though the state remains subordinate to colonial power (Chatterjee 1993a: 5–6; Sethi 1999: 71).

Postcolonial studies can also be held responsible for another of the nation's pitfalls: it advocates that nation-formation as well as the discourse of nationalism enlists the role of elite players who create marginalized and subaltern groups. But here again, one would have to take on board the mutation of the nation's subjects in the growth towards nationhood and the advantages of a discourse of unification over one of difference (Chrisman 2004: 189). Within the allegedly homogeneous discourse of nationalism, there can exist enough room for the activities of subordinated groups. Although postcolonial studies argues persuasively on the subject of patriarchal tendencies, not all political struggles, consciously or otherwise, tend to subordinate its minorities. The neglect of both the nation's subalterns (Spivak 1995: xi) and its women (Parker et al. 1992: 7), who are believed to be abandoned after the nationalist project reaches its proper conclusion, may not be reduced to being another of the many ills of the ideology of nationalism. In the case of women, for example, they have clearly contributed along with men to a variety of political struggles, which have generated emancipatory possibilities.[17] Critics of nationalism pay scant attention to the rapid globalization of postcolonial countries that have tended to corrupt the positive aspects of nationalism. For all their defects, national movements and nationalism do have their strengths, such as insisting on the right to citizenship or the concept of state (if not individual) freedom. Above all, the fulfilment of nationalist struggles does create a climate for a greater historical sense, for a sense of self-worth and civilizational consciousness, and for the eradication of illiteracy among the people. As Aimé Césaire has pointed out:

> I have always thought that the black man was searching for his identity. And it has seemed to me that if what we want is to establish this identity, then we must have a concrete consciousness of what we are – that is, of the first fact of our lives: that we are black; that we were black and have a history, a history that contains certain cultural elements of great value; and that Negroes were not ... born yesterday, because there have been beautiful and important black civilizations ... [W]e affirmed that we were Negroes and that we were proud of it, and that we thought that Africa was not some sort of blank page in the history of humanity. (Césaire 1972: 76)[18]

The formation of the nation, for Césaire, is a historic possibility, a guarantee of liberty and an assertion of selfhood. Exceedingly activist and confrontational, postcolonialism's ancestral figures serve as reminders that colonialism, decolonization and the significance of the nation are predominantly postcolonial preoccupations that cannot be dismissed in the interest of diasporic consciousness.

The postcolonial objection that nationalism is 'derivative' may also be circumvented if the nationalist enterprise is identified with projects relating to local struggles and forms of resistance.[19] In African and Asian societies, nationalism is believed to have been a consequence of the importation of western ideas into a native ethos by the educated elite (Chatterjee 1986). Having long combated forms of European racism, the educated bourgeoisie provide the spur to national movements in the greater part of the third world. However, postcolonial studies, in its preoccupation with anti-colonial nationalism, tends to disregard alternative histories that pose a series of interruptions in the conceptualization of a homogeneous cultural identity, and highlights the difficulties of translating ideology into history within the national struggle. During the Indian national movement, instances of peasant struggles which were initiated for material rather than cultural gains are well known. The nature of these struggles undermines the depoliticized representations of language, religion, race, caste and gender that are central to a postcolonial critique of the nation. These campaigns for change were national too, and went on regardless of other larger and well-transmitted nationwide political activity such as the Non-cooperation movement of the 1920s, the Civil Disobedience Movement of the 1930s or the Quit India Movement of the 1940s. The Bardoli struggle in Gujarat (1927–29), which owed its origin to an enormous increase in the payment of land revenue, in fact took impetus from constructive activities which were prevalent in the area even after the Non-cooperation movement had been called off. This enabled Congress leaders like Sardar Patel to champion the peasants' cause and take the movement closer to *swaraj* or home-rule. Again, the 1,500 mile march by the Andhra farmers in 1938, which took over a hundred days, had the legislative backing of the Congress. In cases where the workers were employed in British-owned enterprises, the support of the nationalist intelligentsia was much greater since the protest could be conveniently consolidated with anti-imperialism.[20] In spite of all the ambiguities and confusions of mass mobilization, and the manoeuvres of the leadership, nationalist sentiment itself formed a very small part of peasant struggles, although it may be admitted that the national movement certainly provided an environment germane to the cause of the peasants. As for third-world nationalisms having western origins, the argument relates to the small percentage of the intelligentsia that entered the western education system from which nationalism as an idea could have been imbibed. Nationalism, upon examination, turns out to be derived from causes that are material, cultural, bourgeois and even popular.

For instance, in his study of Chauri Chaura, Shahid Amin gives an account of the making of nationalist narratives based on the inconsistencies between the nationalist archive, popular perception and local recall (Amin 1996). The Chauri Chaura incident of February 1922, hugely popularized during the national struggle, involved 'rioting' in which 23 policemen were hacked to death and a police station set ablaze by the locals of Chotki Dumri. In retaliation, the policemen fired at the mob of 'volunteers'. The latter ironically chanted 'Long Live Mahatma Gandhi' amidst the 'rioting', while Gandhi, the advocate of peace, called off the nationwide Non-cooperation movement in condemnation of their undisciplined violence. Decades after the incident, the history of this very episode becomes the 'Chauri Chaura *kand* [event]', recounting the outrage committed on the 'accredited freedom fighters' who were fired at indiscriminately. In a 1972 account of the incident described in the 'History of Freedom Struggle in the Gorakhpur District', the men from Chotki Dumri are taken to have assembled at the police station to 'commemorate' the 'martyrdom' of others who had previously been shot dead by the police. As Amin writes: 'The nationalist telescoping of chronology here reaches its temporal limit. A crowd which lost at least three of its members to the police firing of 4 February is here assembled to protest an incident which is yet to happen!' (Amin 1996: 55). Likewise, Gandhi's policy of boycotting depots of foreign cloth dutifully displaces the actual looting of meat, fish and liquor by the rioters. As for those who masterminded the boycott, the District History does not so much as mention them. In present-day Chauri Chaura, there exist two memorials: one honours Mahatma Gandhi, Moti Lal Nehru and Indira Gandhi, but nowhere refers to those of Dumri who were killed, hanged or convicted; the other is the Chauri Chaura memorial, originally built by the British to commemorate the dead policemen, which has now been 'nationalized' and re-engraved as a monument to those very policemen (Amin 1996: 198–200).

Through close readings, Amin demonstrates how the Chauri Chaura incident attained national proportions, even though it had been condemned at the time, and in spite of the peasant-volunteers who were turned into 'hooligans' and 'criminals' soon after the event. Years later, this piece of nationalist history fails even to remember correctly those who were participants in it. The various kinds of testimony that Amin gathers of the events of February 1922 from local memory highlight a wide discrepancy between definitive and remembered history, a discrepancy that makes room for exaggeration, distortion and evasion. Seen independently of cultural constructs, the local accounts show the face of popular nationalism: the atrocities committed against the policemen and the acts of looting were all accounted for in the name of *swaraj*. What Amin shows us, in effect, is an 'enmeshed, intertwined and imbricated web of narratives from every available source' in order to intervene in the official records (Amin 1996: 194). The popular reconstruction of Chauri Chaura makes nationalism's 'derivative' status suspect, at best.

Postcolonial theories of nationalism would thus have to include views that suggest alternatives to their devaluation of existing parameters and yet be critical of their own conveniently held positions. Exile, migration and various forms of dislocation alone are not symptomatic of postcolonialism though they may dominate contemporary postcolonial studies. Although these categories obfuscate themes of being and belonging to a territory in terms of national allegiance, they cannot always undo or reverse discourses against imperialism – as in Palestine, Cuba or Brazil – that proclaim themselves nationalist. The creation of conceptual categories of exile and deterritoriality can eliminate neither the possibility of straightforward resistance outside discourse nor the shrill assertions of ethnic core values and identities we are witnessing today that silence the interplay between the two worlds. It is the anxieties of the 'free world' that have given rise to incipient and narrow nationalisms witnessed to different degrees in India, Serbia and many Islamic countries which then become a subject of debate in postcolonial studies – although such 'parochialism', it must be admitted, may be the only mode of countering American intervention:

> [I]t seems to me that 'a certain nationalism' *is* fundamental in the 'Third World'. It is fundamental, arguably, because it is today and for the foreseeable future still only on the inherited terrain of the *nation* that an articulation between secular intellectualism and popular consciousness can be forged; and *this* is important, in turn, because in the era of transnational capitalism it is only on the basis of such a universalistic articulation – that is, on the basis of nationalitarian struggle – that it is possible to imagine a postcapitalist world order. (Lazarus 1997: 46)

As against the historically grounded nation-state, contemporary postcolonial theorists like Bhabha advocate a 'separation from origins and essences' in relation to the construction of national space (Bhabha 1994: 120). Simply put, Bhabha's formulation implies an isolation from the local, the national and the indigenous that not only makes the totalizing authority of the nation-state uncertain but also downplays resistance. The closest he comes to establishing a site for resistance is when he erodes the direct relationship between power and knowledge through the parody implicit in the doubleness of the native voice (Bhabha 1994: 112).[21] Bhabha thereby divorces his argument from any historical context or political location in deference to a narrative in which resistance has a dubious presence. A series of aggressive questions in Bhabha's essay, 'The Commitment to Theory' explain his intent:

> Must we always polarize in order to polemicize? Are we trapped in a politics of struggle where the representation of social antagonisms and historical contradictions can take no other form than a binarism of theory vs politics? Can the aim of freedom of knowledge be the simple inversion of the relation of oppressor and oppressed, centre and periphery, negative image and positive image? Is our only way out of such dualism the espousal of an implacable oppositionality or the invention of an originary counter-myth of radical purity? (Bhabha 1994: 19).

Bhabha argues that the notion of hybridity in a globalized climate negates the existence of all kinds of identity – national, ethnic, class – and dispenses with commitment to an ethic. In the same way, Gilroy's arguments against culturally absolute categories like the nation can be sustained only within a culture of 'instability and mutability of identity'. Nowhere does Gilroy lament the loss of economic possibilities or class struggle as he sketches out a programme for a 'compound culture' of black people around the world (Gilroy 1993: xi, 15).[22] Postmodernist critics will undoubtedly find the interrogation of national categories of the 'pure' and the 'indigenous' a cause to celebrate not only because linearity and totality are here disavowed but also because room for the new narrative of globalization can be created in the ambiguous spaces that remain after the nation is critiqued.[23] For such critics, the story of the birth of the nation must be accompanied by its inevitable ruptures and confusions, where the metaphors of hybridity and decomposition become more significant than any kind of authoritative orthodoxy. Marxist critics, however, will see in this wholly discursive concern a kind of complicity with contemporary globalization.

III

Indeed, the receding vision of the nation from the third world in the face of globalization becomes one of the primary reasons for a greater defence of native cultures. Since globalization is synonymous with migration and dispossession, the historic possibility inherent in the idea of the nation has largely disappeared. With that have also dissipated agency, empowerment and confrontation. So what do we have now in its place? Perhaps 'a community of the "unhomely", a new internationalism, a gathering of people in the diaspora' (Hardt and Negri 2000: 145). Hardt and Negri's estimation of the nation-state in their widely discussed book, *Empire*, forms part of my discussion, though more by way of disagreement than conciliation, with a view to arriving at the political relevance of the nation-state today.

Elsewhere, in a lesser-known article, 'Globalization and Democracy', published after *Empire*, Hardt and Negri maintain that globalization does not result in the demise of the nation-state. In the areas of governance relating to economics, politics and culture it continues to be important although it has been 'displaced from the position of sovereign authority' (Hardt and Negri 2003: 109). For the two authors, a substitution of 'nation' by 'Empire' has taken place which creates a 'new form of sovereignty' (Hardt and Negri 2003: 109), one which is borderless because it combines in itself three forms of government – monarchy, aristocracy and democracy. Their explanation of these forms appears to be ironic but is not so. The United States is the monarch, indisputable master of the world, ruling through the Pentagon, the institution symbolizing its military might. The big three – the World Trade Organization, the World Bank and the International Monetary Fund – are in the service of securing US monarchy. The Empire is aristocratic in the sense that only a select few (like the G8 and the UN Security Council) are in control of the rest of the world. Once again, they are aided by the transnational corporations and their exclusivist practices. As for democracy, the US-led nations and the developing world can together appropriate Empire's democratic function by being representative of their people. The United Nations General Assembly is the primary example here. If all else fails, we can always fall back on non-governmental organizations that proclaim emphatically the democratic roots of all nation-states. With these three strands, the new state that is the Empire can include within itself collaboration and dissent, similarity and difference.

The nation-states may appear to be facing a crisis in their ability to administer 'economic and cultural exchanges', but that is largely owing to their replacement by 'Empire' (Hardt and Negri 2000: xii). Having adjusted to the strength of global capital, Empire will, the two authors believe, supersede not just the nation-state but the United States as well. In all of this, national and cultural boundaries will cease to matter: 'the Empire is a kind of smooth space across which subjectivities glide without substantial resistance or conflict' (Hardt and Negri 2000: 198). Bhabha's opposition of dialectical binaries is symptomatic of the passage from 'nation' to 'Empire' which is the 'epochal shift' witnessed in the world today (Hardt and Negri 2000: 145). The ideology of Empire is inimical to both the fictions of nationalism and the interstitial spaces of cultural difference. Unlike postcolonial theorists who demystify the existence of a nationalist sentiment, or the reality of an uncorrupted nation (in its notional sense), the authors of *Empire* insist that the challenge to homogenization is simply not enough. In 'Globalization and Democracy' they write: 'One would presumably have to develop a notion of the global people that extends beyond any national or ethnic conception to unite the entirety of humanity' (Hardt and Negri 2003: 112).

Quite obviously, Hardt and Negri are far from addressing the nation-states of the developing world, those that had declared themselves sovereign after their decolonization struggles and now find themselves under pressure of globalization. As for these less fortunate states, they were 'never really sovereign': 'The entry into modernity for many nation-states was the entry into relations of economic and political subordination that undercut any sovereignty to which the nation might pretend' (Hardt and Negri 2003: 110). Hardt and Negri further argue that since the sovereignty of the nation-state depends upon the sovereignty of the people or the 'multitude', the concept of the people becomes important. At the same time, the people have a more demotic than real significance, that is, they are the representation of a unity rather than actually being united. The illusory complexion of the 'proletariat' heightens further when nation gives way to Empire. If the Empire consists of transnational corporations, one would have to agree with Hardt and Negri that it can scarcely support the sentiments of the people. After the Second World War and the dissolution of imperialism, it was the multitude that brought the modern world to the point of postmodernity and to the new era of decentred capital. This new borderless world, pursuing the end of capital accumulation without obstruction, was responsible for the end of the nation-state.

But for the states that came into being following decolonization struggles, state power and state sovereignty derive largely from the power constituted in them by the people who make the state truly democratic. However, in practice, the United States did not itself follow this democratic principle. It was perhaps the first to make democracy compatible with class rule as well as the first to institute the two separate realms of the economic and the political so characteristic of capitalism (Meiksins Wood 2003: 76). The concept of democracy that Hardt and Negri attribute to the US is symptomatic of an authorial prejudice for forms of governance practiced there. The form of democracy that the Founding Fathers of the United States originally conceived was borrowed from Greek political thought – where the people are a significant entity though certainly not free of elite control – but redefined regularly so as eventually to connote a state of 'democracy' where even the suspension of civil liberties would not be taken as a sign of the infringement of constitutional rights (Meiksins Wood 2003: 79).

The original modern state – a consequence of Renaissance humanism but often used since as a repressive mechanism to homogenize difference – differs sharply from the states of developing countries. In the context of developing countries, the nation-state (as we know it) assumed enormous significance in overthrowing colonialism. So long as decolonized countries worked on a socialist model, the nation-state remained strong. But with the delegitimization of the ideology of socialist states, the impetus towards capitalism grew. The outward signs of good fortune tend to eclipse the desire for freedom from global forces inherent in nation-states. The greater the global pressures, the lesser the status of nation-states in the developing world. In other words, the greater the expansion of the economy, the greater the shrinking of the political will and the means of political control. Currently, the state refuses to deal with key aspects connected with the economy for fear of reprisals from the world markets. The states thus render themselves ineffective, submitting to what Ken Jowitt calls the 'new world disorder' (see Jowitt 1992). The phenomenon of the diminishing nation-state is a consequence of its own industrial growth as foreign capital investment begins to exercise power over it and serves to keep the economy free from government intervention. The weakness of nation-states has reached the point where there is almost a complete relinquishment of regulatory control, subordinating all anti-capitalist policies to the mood of the market.[24] Globalization is thus not just an inexorable, irresistible current of capitalism but, more than that, the consequence of choices made by heads of state who seem untroubled by the ruin of local economies by global business.

No doubt capitalism contains within itself the possibility of segregating its economic from its political functions. It is for this reason and this alone that capital has expanded without limits. Capitalism's economic mode enables it to expand in relation to growing consumerism and free itself to a large extent from the sovereignty of the state. Notwithstanding this, the state must retain the role of administrator holding the economy accountable to its people through an elaborate system of taxation, regulated trade, negotiations of rates of interest, control over currency exchanges and so on. The state is still needed to impose law and taxation, and to provide public health, education and security for which there is still no other comparable institution. Meiksins Wood draws attention to the fact that globalization has 'extended capital's purely economic powers far beyond the range of any single nation-state' which means that 'global capital requires *many* nation-states to perform the necessary administrative and coercive functions' (Meiksins Wood 2003: 68). Neither the WTO nor the IMF can take over these functions of the state; it is the nation-state that maintains the legal and political systems required to control the ebb and flow of capital. Despite the seductions of globalization, the inbuilt defence mechanism of the nation-state to protect itself from exploitation by foreign interests can always be put to work.

In developing their arguments, Hardt and Negri overlook the contribution made by nation-states in introducing and controlling the degree of globalization in their local cultures; indeed, it can be argued that the 'essence of globalization is not the declining capacity but the unique *ability* of nation-states to organize the world for global capital' (Meiksins Wood 2003: 65). The rise of nation-states from the ashes of the Soviet Union, wherein ethnic societies had been subjugated by a single-party government, is one example negating the belief in the demise of nation-states. Again, the European Union itself has arisen on the basis of the solidity of individual states. Even leaving that aside, there are many aboriginal, marginalized or separatist groups who want their own state.[25] 'Internationalization', as discussed by Hardt and Negri, can in hindsight be interpreted as referring to more than simply the embrace of globalization. In fact, it imbues the nation-state with power.

In the present scenario of the decolonized world, nation-states should assume even more power, particularly if they can support local struggles against the excesses of global capital. This might be capitalism's nemesis, or at least the only way to effectively put a check on it. The view that globalization has swallowed up states should thus be re-assessed considering that political organization of any sort can ultimately only be achieved through the nation-state, particularly with regard to struggles against massive capital inflows that create global asymmetries. Far from sounding the obitural note for the state, it would not be incorrect to say that the state remains equally significant for both the proponents and the enemies of neoliberalism. It may even be the prize in the tug of war between the promoters and the detractors of globalization. That is why governments become the 'key zone of contestation' (Mertes 2003: 146), and are pilloried from either side. Examples of protests from all over Latin America and parts of the developing world (which I enumerate in the following chapter), after states opened their gates to foreign investment, are ample testimony to its primacy: for example, the Peruvian struggle to resist the privatization of electricity; the 'water wars' in Bolivia that became the bane of Banzer's rule in 2000; the mobilization of the people of Ecuador against deforestation and the privatization of electricity and oil; and the BJP-led agitation in India against the setting up of the Enron power plant to supply electricity when its economic viability was in question. When a whole new 'Ministry of Disinvestment' was created by the BJP government itself when it came into power in 1998, on the premise that there would be a 'direct link between privatisation and social needs', there were demonstrations and protests across India.[26] In all these instances, the government was taken to task because it was playing a role in the globalization process and because the loyalists, so we might call them, put their trust in the state to roll back its policies. The state, thus, can be both the enemy and the safeguard.

One cannot rule out the potential capacity for resistance of nation-states in the developing world: in Asian countries where governments have been successful in holding on to nationalized institutions by preventing the infiltration of foreign investment, the state continues to be an important phenomenon. The controls imposed by the Malaysian government during the 1997–98 financial crisis protected them from the experience of economic collapse experienced by Indonesia. It is no wonder that the demand for separate nation-states is also steadily growing. This goes along with the understanding, however, that sooner or later the pressure from Washington to reduce barriers to international trade and allow easy admittance to American businesses, thus subjecting domestic industry to the risk of severe competition from abroad, will have to be met.

Whereas postcolonial theorists question the meaning of the nation today as a culturally imagined unity, Marxists remain confident of the power evinced in resistance movements which can come only from nation-states. An analysis of nation-states grounded in historical materialism can certainly animate postcolonial critiques of homogeneous national configurations and reconceive them in relation to resistance, revolution, or even an internationalism grounded in local struggles. Unfortunately, in the light of postcolonial studies, globalization itself is considered a discourse – global*ism*, more likely – or simply a fantasy or ideology that 'acts as if a "borderless world" has already been accomplished for capitalism, realizing in fantasy what has not yet been (and cannot – within capitalism – be) materially achieved' (Bartolovich 2000: 134). To follow Hardt and Negri, who are more 'postcolonial' than the postcolonialists, is to surrender to globalization as an inexorable and inevitable force that would result in discrediting the continuing presence of the nation-state and the role played by the socialist left in subaltern struggles. Nations and nation-states have not completely lost their viability since all forms of protest, resistance and revolution continue to be linked with national liberation movements and ideologies (Debray 1977: 26). The belief in nationhood may still have potential if one is able to move beyond the assumption that nationalist discourse is reactionary and that theories of diasporic globalism have wiped out any belief in national identity. As Fanon memorably wrote: 'It is at the heart of national consciousness that international consciousness lives and grows' (Fanon 1967: 199).

What, then, should governments do? Hardly any government can reject globalization altogether. There is a difficult middle course most nation-states have to take between free trade and protectionism, a kind of 'social democratic corporatism' which enables states to keep their autonomy while also benefiting from globalization, working on the principle that markets can be global even as politics is national (Garrett 2004: 235). The social corporatism model advocates the primacy of the public sector in which social security, redistribution schemes and other benefits are not lost in service to the stock market. Mindless privatization of core sectors and public services, reckless liberalization and disinvestment of profitable enterprises, have to be avoided at all costs in order to ensure a happy medium between the local and the global. The recent examples of Brazil, Bolivia and Argentina provide evidence of the swing from neoliberalism to broad-based ground-level struggles. A sign of Brazilian resistance to the US was evinced in 2002 when former President Luiz Lula da Silva, soon after his election, cancelled a deal to purchase 24 new fighter planes for the Brazilian air force (Rohter 2002). The money saved, which amounted to $750 million, was used for hunger-eradication programmes (Johnson 2004: 280). In Venezuela, the Bolivarian Alliance of the Americas led by President Hugo Chávez is again an instance of a government involving people in the economic, social and political schemes intended to support the underprivileged and rebuild the economy free of neoimperialism.[27] Nation-states like these are not merely attempting to salvage something from the debris of state socialism, they are involved in building a historical reality that will help them recover from the oppression of contemporary global capitalism.

3

GLOBALIZATION AND PROTEST

I

It is clear from our discussion in the previous chapter that for the decolonized world, there is nothing 'post' about colonialism and that the issue of identities, in terms of representation, race and gender, is still not resolved. Yet the term 'postcolonial' has replaced 'colonial' so rapidly, it is as though political decolonization marked the cessation of economic and cultural domination as well. As a consequence, the employment of the 'post' in academic circles and its absence in the world outside has been observed and criticized, bringing theory and practice head to head. Unless abstract theory translates itself into action and real events, and is productively employed in materialist history, postcolonial studies cannot claim to be political. Bereft of rigour and radicalism, it retreats into passivity and becomes reduced to a classroom study of concepts like hybridity and hyphenation which do not promise anything more than plain pedagogy. This chapter highlights modes of protest which I suggest should be included within the rubric of postcolonial studies to give it meaning. What makes this discussion even more urgent is the growing impoverishment of more than half the world's population, increasing civil strife, international tension and the nameless spectre of terrorism, all of which constitute serious reasons for desiring some kind of political reaction from the postcolonial academy.

It is no coincidence that postcolonial studies originated with the growth of capitalism and its rapid expansion in the world. The links between globalization and postcolonialism were strengthened as postcolonial studies in the academy became institutionalized to analyse colonization and the rise of eurocentric tendencies, both of which are related to capital investment. By the time US academia decided to take postcolonialism on board, themes relating to the relationship between capital accumulation and migrancy, travel and exile, had become trademark postcolonial studies. As will be argued in the following chapter on postcolonialism and the United States, the migration of third-world intellectuals to western universities as a result of capital expansion, and the subsequent growth of 'theory' as a consumer durable with a limited shelf life bolstered by postmodernist thought, are unrelated to any enhancement in the real lives of the people. This may be the reason why postcolonial theory, in particular, is accused of being implicated in the project of global capitalist neoliberalism. When postcolonialism enters university curricula as postcolonial studies, which includes a range of topics such as the problematic of language, history as representation, nation as monolith, constructions of gender and race, multiculturalism, hybridity and the diasporic sensibility, it is seen as part of the west's agenda to undermine the margins.

The concurrence between postcolonial studies and globalization develops from the substitution of the 'homogeneous Eurocentric narrative of development and social change' by a 'transnational' cultural world order (Gikandi 2001: 628). Both narratives emerge from the post-Enlightenment phase of history. The former, based on the traditional world-system theory used to analyse unequal development, considers globalization to be a chronological product of the homogenizing journey of modernization of which the formation of the nation-state is a part. But the latter is unmoored from the centre–periphery model of the world and constitutes the romance, albeit far too overstated, of a free-flowing discourse and an economy detached from imperial control. Postcolonial studies prospers from the second narrative of globalization with its generous use of the culturalist terminology of hybridity and displacement. But critics of the transnational version of globalization will not easily abandon the binaries of core and periphery or give up their disapproval of the stark divisions it creates in society. They juxtapose globalization with further westernization and a sense of doom. It is within this context that the nation is believed to have failed its citizens with its inability to check modernization in the new guise of globalization. This is also the failure of postcolonialism in not offering safeguards and instead joining forces with the enemy. The academicization of postcolonialism, the suspicion of the narrative of the nation, and the rapid globalization of the world converge on one aspect, that is, they are complicit in pushing grassroots reality to a distant horizon.[1] If postcolonialism is to remain concerned with the empowerment of the so-called third world, it should disengage itself from any kind of unilateralism of the west.

The emergence of nation-states would itself have been a form of enablement had it not been for the very globality of its conception. By the middle of the twentieth century, it was clear that the process of decolonization that had begun in the previous century was irrevocable and that nation-states would become 'the most desirable, viable, and legitimate way of structuring political life' (Lechner and Boli 2004: 211). But the process of nation-building would be one in which most postcolonial states would end up becoming subservient to new forms of imperialism and hegemonies. Jawaharlal Nehru, independent India's first prime minister, spoke in his midnight speech about India's 'tryst with destiny' (1947), echoed years later, ironically, by Rushdie in *Midnight's Children*, with the premonition that the dreams of the new nation would remain unconsummated:

> There was an extra festival on the calendar, a new myth to celebrate, because a nation which had never previously existed was about to win its freedom, catapulting us into a world which, although it had five thousand years of history, although it had invented the game of chess and traded with Middle Kingdom Egypt, was nevertheless quite imaginary; into a mythical land, a country which would never exist except by the efforts of a phenomenal collective will – except in a dream we all agreed to dream; it was a mass fantasy ... and would periodically need the sanctification and renewal which can only be provided by rituals of blood. (Rushdie 1980: 129–30)

As with many of his contemporaries, Nehru's orientation and attitudes remained primarily western as India was taken over by a top-heavy infrastructure closely resembling the one that had existed during its 200 years of colonization.[2] Fanon is perhaps the most prophetic of all theorists of nationalism in his denunciation of the 'wilful narcissism' of the nationalist middle class, of which Nehru is an example, that replaces the abstract policies of the departed colonialist with the 'sterile formalism' of a national consciousness that seldom includes social and political awareness.[3]

As decolonization became almost simultaneous with the worldwide growth of trade, the ingress of capital into third-world markets which had begun with the onset of colonialism continued unabashedly thereafter. Not for nothing had Cabral said in the context of Guinea-Bissau: 'The *liberation struggle is a revolution* and ... it does not finish at the moment when the national flag is raised and the national anthem played' (Cabral 1966: n.p.). The processes of globalization, which have their roots in older models of imperialism, are an ongoing form of neocolonialism, as is corroborated by one of the earliest and perhaps the most sophisticated analysts of neocolonialism, Kwame Nkrumah, the first president of independent Ghana, who proclaimed: 'The essence of neocolonialism is that the State which is subject to it is, in theory, independent and has all the outward trappings of international sovereignty. In reality its economic system and thus political policy is directed from outside' (Nkrumah 1965: n.p.). Neocolonialism receives its impetus mainly from newly independent nation-states that invest in industrial programmes initiated by multinational corporations (mostly set up in these very nation-states which, in turn, contribute to environmental degradation) aided by the International Monetary Fund, the World Bank, the International Bank of Settlements in Basle or the OECD (Organization for Economic Cooperation and Development) in order to embrace modernity and development in their willingness to stride ahead. The IMF and the World Bank lend huge sums of money to these countries in return for unfettered trade conditions, removal of local subsidies and the privatization of public amenities. New nation-states that are unable to honour the loans fall prey to mountains of debt. This is one of the ways in which so-called developing countries succumb to a continual subordination to their former masters. As a consequence, the promises of the national liberation project – the complete freedom of the people from outside governance and control – are defeated.

It is in this sense that Gikandi's argument about globalization as a state of 'crisis', rather than one of 'celebration', is tenable (Gikandi 2001: 629). As we witness the underbelly of globalization through the colossal inequality between rich and poor, there is a sense of disconnection from postcolonial studies, not only because of its inefficacy in reaching out to the underprivileged through its critique but also because of its endorsement of an entire terminology of variables related to the 'diaspora' that disaffiliates the postcolonial intellectual from his/her national moorings when the latter are most required. Globalization, from the traditional linear view, has insidious intentions: western progress comes at the cost of a steady decline in advancement in non-western countries, and it is expedient for western economies to make sure that the situation remains as such so that a corresponding 'dependency' upon western powers ensures their continued material and technological superiority (Amin 1977; 1988). Dependency theories work on the principle that the developing world is purposefully led into economic ruin when its states collaborate with economically rich countries who own the modes of production to create conditions of market expansion. But the huge debts thereby incurred push the developing nation-states over the edge. The forces of globalization are relentless as capitalism's surpluses tend to spill over into the non-capitalist world, thus demonstrating the age-old maxim that imperialism remains 'the political expression of the accumulation of capital in its competitive struggle for what remains still open in the non-capitalist environment' (Luxemburg 1951: 446). A simple substitution of 'imperialism' with 'globalization' indicates the implications of the spread of capitalism which has made the United States the centre of imperial power aided by other rich countries of the north.

Dependency theories end up blaming the advanced nations for all the economic misfortunes of the developing world and, as such, have met with resistance from academic quarters since they neglect 'counter-examples of agency and self-transformation'

(Young 2001: 54). It is also debatable whether centre and margins are quite as easily distinguishable in terms of ongoing economic activity today. Japan is a case in point. Equally, Portugal, once a pre-eminent colonial power, is today only peripheral to the European Union. China and India are also rapidly becoming booming economies thereby undermining the viability of theories that rely on north-south paradigms. But despite the shrill rhetoric of a borderless world and the claims that centre and periphery are no longer water-tight, it has to be admitted that polarization is on the increase. While it can be debated as to whether the centre is 'as heterogeneous and unstable' as the periphery (Moore-Gilbert 1997: 194), mere theoretical gestures cannot alter the reality on the ground.

Dependency theories cannot be eliminated altogether since the world is witness to 'core' industries profiting at the expense of nature and of the ecosystems of the 'periphery'. Gikandi's spectre of the dark side of globalization may then be invoked to describe the excesses of globalization as the new imperialism of the times whereby leading capitalist countries, through the use of supranational institutions, make clients of the developing world. After Mikhail Gorbachev's initiative in introducing capitalism into the USSR, with his famed rhetoric of *glasnost* and *perestroika*, it did not take long for the United States to step in and pick up the pieces. By the time Boris Yeltsin replaced Gorbachev as the chief architect of this capitalist revolution, the World Bank and the IMF moved in strategically to provide 'incentives' and 'aid' programmes intended to stabilize the economic upheaval. As well as clearing millions of dollars worth of Soviet debts, enormous loans were also sanctioned. Aid was given in the form of consultation services that quickly programmed the fall of public enterprises. Jeffrey Sachs, a development economist then at Harvard University – who in 1985 had advised the Bolivian government to downsize government subsidies and dispense with quotas to cure an ailing economy – was among the distinguished intellectuals who were handpicked for the job. Critics, however, believe that Sachs left the Bolivian economy worse off than before – though he helped to curb inflation, he also left behind a legacy of rising unemployment and falling GDP from which Bolivia could never recover.[4] In a similar manner, the 'incentives' given to Russia to facilitate the process of switching over to capitalism were 'tragic' in their effects: welfare-state programmes were abandoned, labour initiatives severely restrained, living standards reduced, health services expropriated and sovereignty reigned in (Aronowitz 2003: 192). The Russian government was faced with the only alternative available to it: denationalization.[5]

The pressures of debt lead to the forced acceptance of the 'structural adjustment programmes' of the creditors, a mere 'euphemism for social austerity' (Aronowitz 2003: 180), but which implies abiding by policy changes in tune with the dictates of the western superpowers, particularly the United States. Under the structural adjustment programmes, duties on imports are lowered while subsidies on one's own produce are removed. The state is also forced to privatize its public-sector undertakings, eliminate trade unionism, and suspend the marketing boards which ensure fair pricing for indigenous commodities. When the west exports its cheap food supplies to developing countries, they invariably ruin the small businesses of these countries. With the farmers then being left with no choice but to migrate to cities, local agriculture gradually meets its demise. Such, then, are the implications of unfettered trade, worked out in partnership between the leaders of the developed and the developing countries. The Agreement on Agriculture, for instance, initiated by the World Trade Organization, forces members of developing countries to curtail tariffs on food imports by 24 per cent for a term of ten years. The AoA also allows western countries to export their commodities very cheaply to developing countries, which edges out local farmers from the competition since they cannot even square their costs of production. In the exercise of these policies, the consumer prices remain the same (Sardar and Davies 2002: 75).[6] All this is done under the garb of economic freedom, free trade and neoliberalism: 'What a country gets out of such a melange of "reforms" is not economic recovery, long-term growth or stability but a government so weakened that it usually declines into a kleptocracy and experiences frequent economic collapses' (Johnson 2004: 267). This is the story of the financial collapse of Mexico in 1994–95, Thailand, South Korea and Indonesia in 1997, Brazil and Russia in 1998, Argentina in 2000 and Venezuela in 2002. Severe economic crises precipitated by structural adjustment programmes compelled these countries to depend increasingly on US corporations for consumer durables, jobs and public amenities.[7]

As for US imperialism, Mill's view of British colonies in the year 1848, summed up in his book, *Principles of Political Economy*, could well describe its intents and purposes today:

> These are hardly to be looked upon as countries, carrying on an exchange of commodities with other countries, but more properly as outlying agricultural or manufacturing establishments belonging to a larger community. Our West Indian colonies, for example, cannot be regarded as countries, with a productive capital of their own ... [but] the place where England finds it convenient to carry on the production of sugar, coffee and a few other tropical commodities. All the capital employed is English capital; almost all the industry is carried on for English uses; there is little production of anything except for staple commodities, and these are sent to England, not to be exchanged for things exported to the colony and consumed by its inhabitants, but to be sold in England for the benefit of the proprietors there. The trade with the West Indies is hardly to be considered as external trade, but more resembles the traffic between town and country, and is amenable to the principles of the home trade. (Mill 1965: 693)

Unquestionably, globalization had existed even during the traditional phase of colonial activity accompanied by the profiteering ambitions of Europe's many companies operating in the east. More than a 160 years after Mill, his comments have an apt bearing on the imperialist policies of the United States that are designed to 'hemorrhage' profits from direct US investments (Galeano 1997: 207).[8] The collapse of third-world economies is now scripted by policies relating to trade liberalization and by favouring foreign companies with higher levels of ownership in those economies. The financial collapse of Thailand was the consequence of conditions enforced by the International Monetary Fund that operates as a subservient body to the designs of the

United States.[9] The US was able to exercise power over many of Thailand's banks and financial institutions thanks to its owning larger equity. We can say, following Hoogvelt, that 'the scope and detail of the combined IMF conditionality rules and the World Bank structural adjustment contracts have amounted to a degree of economic intervention in debtor countries which [match], perhaps even [exceed] the direct administration of bygone colonial governments' (Hoogvelt 1997: 167).

The WTO[10] replaced GATT (its forerunner until 1994), mainly in order to push away the ladder in order to prevent developing countries from catching up (Johnson 2004: 271).[11] From Friedrich List (1856) to Joseph Stiglitz (2002), historical accounts provide enough evidence that globalization is always at the cost of third-world prosperity. The benefits of international trade treaties and the triumphalism of free markets, which the United States never tires of broadcasting, are in practice inequitable to the third world.[12] Yet President George W. Bush maintained during his tenure that free markets and free trade 'proved their ability to lift whole societies out of poverty – so the United States is working with the entire global trading community to build a world that trades in freedom and therefore grows in prosperity' (Bush 2002). Globalization is a means to create this supposed ladder of economic success and disguise its removal in such a manner that the majority of the population of the world, both in the advanced west, but even more so in the third world, are eliminated from 'the emerging "thickening" network of human, social and economic interaction. Rather than being an expansive process, the present process of globalisation appears to be an imploding or shrinking one' (Hoogvelt 1997: 84).

And still we speak of the distinction between the 'discourses' of globalization and the 'processes' of capital formation (Brah 2002: 31), as if the former, which purportedly include the idealistic universalism of greater egalitarianism, a global levelling of economic relations, democratic give and take and the accompanying freedom, could overpower the latter which are constitutive of the ways and means by which the public sphere can be subordinated by the private. The gap between the 'discourses' and the 'processes' of capital formation exists only as a persuasive argument because what the world gets is not globalization but 'neoliberalism' or 'turbo-capitalism' (Klein 2002b: 46) which creates more inequalities than have ever existed before. Globalization, which is based on the trickle-down effect, has not taken place so far. Thus 'corporatization' becomes a more suitable term to describe 'new areas of ownership' and exclusion (Klein 2002b: 47). Correspondingly, a recurrent theme of globalization is the 'fence' by which third-world countries barricade their institutions against their own people on the advice of the World Bank. Running streams of water become unavailable when Pepsi or Coke decide to set up manufacturing units. Huge infrastructure projects such as the Sardar Sarovar Dam on the river Narmada in India are built by governments at the cost of rendering thousands homeless. In Argentina, the very idea of democracy stands threatened when the IMF rejects requests for loans on the pretext that social spending be reduced and further privatization introduced. State-level barricades have been imposed by multinational seed giants who dictate which genetically modified crops should be grown; US agribusinesses regularly indulge in seed-tampering and patenting which affects natural farming all across the global south by preventing farmers from re-planting existing seeds cheaply. Furthermore, there is a fencing of news, which is why we hardly hear of Africa. There are also 'unvirtual' fences – those made of concrete, steel and razor wire, such as the walls being built in the West Bank – which are instances of strict border controls imposed by wealthy countries.[13] Leaders of the global north hold their summits within moats and barriers to make the conference area inaccessible owing to threats posed by violent protesters. During the Summit of the Americas in Quebec City in 2001, downtown Quebec was completely caged, its residents forced to show proof of identity in order to gain access to their own homes. As a poster in Quebec City declared: 'Capital is enclosure. First it fenced off the land. Then it metered the water. It measured our time. It plundered our bodies and now it polices our dreams. We cannot be contained. We are not for sale' (Notes 2003: 28–9). The G8 summits or the WTO conclaves also usually take place in isolated locations to prevent the ingress of life-threatening terrorists as much as rightful protesters. If it is global policy-makers who erect such fences, then global economic policies cannot be floated as signs of true democracy. Without actually giving the power of taking decisions to the people, 'processes' of capital formation will always be one step ahead of so-called 'discourses' of globalization, a reminder of the failed promise of modernization: 'So instead of more equality what we have is forgotten people, we have forgotten continents. And instead of development we have the dismantling of the social safety net that we had, done in order to facilitate investment' (Klein 2002b: 47). The 'social safety net' is a reference to those policies of the nation-state that are able to impose controls to undermine the processes of globalization.

Instead of exercising a regulatory role, the state tends to allow foreign investments.[14] Few people realize that the Ganges itself has been privatized by the company Suez, a global water giant, resulting in the suspension of all public water supply schemes by the government of India. In order to supply 635 million litres of Ganges water to Delhi's elite, at least 100,000 people will be forcefully evicted from their homes owing to the construction of the Tehri Dam that will aid the venture (Shiva 2005: 78–9). Similarly, few Bolivians knew in the year 2000, when Bolivia leased off Cochabamba's water to a company called Aguas del Tunari until 2039, that they would have to pay more than 200 per cent of the cost of water. Unknown to them, Aguas del Tunari is a subsidiary of Bechtel, one of California's largest engineering corporates. The destruction of the forest cover, damming of river waters and excessive mining creates a chain effect and takes its toll on the ecosystem as nation-states open their doors to the global economy. The arbitrary felling of trees, for instance, has flooded the Sunderbans delta which in turn is responsible for frequent floods in Bangladesh and the extinction of wildlife.[15] In Mexico, widespread deforestation by the TNCs involved in the lumber business destroyed the natural habitat of the Mexican Indians who had to move closer to the US border in an effort to seek jobs. The fall-out was the 1994 rebel uprising in Chiapas.

The discrepancy between the local and the global that capitalism has bred includes rapid changes in the lifestyles of women in developing economies which often leads to both a rejection of modernity and its promotion under forms of economic liberalization. Global capitalism may have favoured female employment, but its temporary and part-time nature has only increased insecurity among women. On examining the employment base, it appears that transnational corporations employ far more women workers than men, primarily because they are regarded as easily replaceable in the global market. Women in the global social system largely consist of low-waged immigrants who bear the brunt of capital accumulation in the hands of a few. The large number of Asian women who work as domestic help in the rich households of developed countries is an indication of the pressures of globalization permeating the circulation of labour.[16] In the corporate system, women, especially those of the developing world, earn less than men; in the agricultural sector, women find themselves removed from time-honoured methods of functioning associated with an agrarian economy as their age-old occupations of treating, classifying and conserving seeds fall into disuse owing to the imposed practice of growing genetically modified crops. The production of cash crops in the nineteenth century under colonial rule, which reversed the methods of traditional agrarian farming, had similarly affected women's traditional concerns, like singing, story telling and herb gathering (Tharu and Lalitha 1995: 148–9). With the departure of indentured labour and with rising urbanization, detachment from the land grew, culminating in the withdrawal from tradition, ritual and ceremony.

The question then arises: how are we to respond to the deep-seated fears and anxieties of the people? Apart from Marxism, which philosophy will take them on board? No doubt theories of interdependence/transculturation which argue for the mutuality of the binaries – colonizer/colonized, master/slave – are extremely significant in raising the issue of the effects of the local upon the global. The arguments offered by Appadurai (2000), Hall (1996), Bhabha (1994), Gilroy (1993) and even the later Said (1993) are compelling in undoing the grand narratives of monolithic structures, but outside their cultural connotations their impact is limited. There is seldom any exploration of the reasons for the easy companionship between postcolonialism and globalization or any interrogation of the way in which the rise of postcolonial studies is contingent on the growth of capital. Even more so, there has been no attempt to intervene in the rapidly increasing industrialization of our times by invoking agency or subjectivity through an uncompromising political stance, as foregrounded in San Juan Jr's commentaries on Rigoberta Menchú and Maria Barros. It is ironic that in his efforts to critique western history, Bhabha argues that the native has a voice only in the splitting of imperial discourse, between the gaps of their enunciation and the site of its address, in the 'excess' and 'slippage' inherent in the replication of their history. Anti-colonial struggles are undoubtedly triggered by colonial aggression and are not independent of it, but to assume that the indigenous response can be no more than a suggestion – so imperceptible as to go almost unnoticed – is to scarcely give the native voice an existence independent of colonialism which emerges, on the other hand, as something of a reified structure (Bhabha 1994: 93–101).[17] Much postcolonial writing works on the premise of the contagion, contamination or corruption of identities, thereby forsaking the active choices made by people in the face of totalitarianism.

II

Outside academic parameters, globalization as a force may be understood in a more economic than cultural sense as a process which the state is both in agreement with and in opposition to. This ties up with the earlier formulation about the intricate relationship between the state and the nation. It is the state which ushers in globalization even as it should be imposing regulatory controls. All this time, the nation hovers like an absent presence over and above the contrariness of the state. As capital flows marginalize the nation-state, postcolonial theory writes the story of the national imaginary, or, following Appadurai, of 'uncertain landscapes' (Appadurai 2000: 1816) unmoored from a pastness which is otherwise so relevant to the nation. But there is another kind of nationalist narrative that is alive and kicking and which reappears in the resurgence of subaltern voices that cannot be contained within the postcolonial nation-space. These voices are part of the 'national' struggle waged by the proletariat against their own bourgeoisie, which is not national in 'substance' but national in 'form' (Marx and Engels 1967: 232). It is here that globalization engenders a 'nation' that is more material than cultural, that exhibits a revolutionary tendency and a reaffirmation of faith in local movements as if to proclaim, with the protesters at the World Social Forum in Porto Alegre, Brazil: 'Another world is possible.' Neither the world-system theories nor transcultural narratives can explain it.

Protest and resistance take on an added urgency in developing countries when neoliberalism, the new guise of globalization, determines 'the nature of the economy a country shall have, what investment shall be undertaken and where, and what kind of development – if any – will take place within ... national borders' (Nyrere, cited in Sivanandan 2004: 58). Nyrere's hard-hitting prognostication finds a parallel in the tenor of the many authors of *We are Everywhere*:

> Ours is the complex task of resisting this power exercised through a web of political, economic and military systems, representing entrenched and often invisible interests. In a global economy, there is no seat of power for the new guerrillas to storm. That is why protestors have been targeting international summit meetings. Unaccountable institutions that determine the fate of the global economy – the World Trade Organization, the World Bank, the International Monetary Fund, the G8, the World Economic Forum – have not been able to meet in recent years without being accompanied by protest. (Notes 2003: 26)

Political activity, even among marginalized groups, has the potential to be an active source of agency within hyperconformism. In Bolivia, there were protests in 2002 against decreased spending on health and education. In El Salvador, similar demonstrations marked the privatization of the Social Security Institute, while in Honduras people rejected a proposed law on drinking water (Alagranati et al. 2004: 123). In Peru, the Fronte Amplio Civico called for a regional strike against the privatization of electricity. Demonstrations in Paraguay took a more national dimension when the Congreso Democrático del Pueblo emerged from existing social and political groups and peasant movements to counter the neoliberal policies of the state that were leading to economic crises. It was a general consensus among such movements that led to the collapse of the WTO summit at Cancún in Mexico in September 2003. Led by Brazil, the Latin Americans demonstrated their resistance to the unilateral policies of the industrialized nations which would have resulted in safeguarding agendas relating to the Free Trade Areas of the Americas in 2005 (Alagranati et al. 2004: 134). The Quebec City summit on negotiating the details of the FTAA was also marked by marches and demonstrations which were anarchical in spirit. Amusingly enough, each protestor was disguised as Robin Hood so that the 34 heads of state, by default, became representative of the authority of the Sheriff of Nottingham.[18] Shouting slogans of 'Robin Hood will be back', the rebels were carried away by the police (Notes 2003: 27).[19]

More notably, in connection with the threat to land rights, the Zapatistas, Mexican rebels of the Chiapas highlands, revolutionized themselves into an army for 12 full days in 1994, fighting the Mexican government's strategies of *neoliberalismo* (Notes 2003: 22). The Zapatista movement has no name just as it has no leadership. And yet it has become the most globalized movement in history despite being anti-globalization in its ideology. Without answers, without legislation or closure, it resembles what the ancient Greeks would have called call an 'aporia', which means not having a 'poros' or a way out (Notes 2003: 506). This is typically the postcolonial predicament. Protests against globalization have largely succeeded as a result of being both nameless and faceless. The resistance movement of the Zapatistas was undoubtedly led by Subcomandante Marcos, but, ironically, he is masked. He is faceless to the extent that anyone who wears a ski mask can call himself Marcos. In many ways, then, the powerful symbol of the mask enables any revolutionary to claim solidarity with Marcos (Notes 2003: 64).

Chiapas is one of Mexico's largest producers of avocados, beef, bananas, cocoa, corn, honey and melons, and is abundant in natural resources. Yet its inhabitants and local population are destitute and malnutritioned. They have neither drinking water nor electricity. Death from poverty and disease is commonplace and education a remote possibility. If not struck down by disease, the average Zapatista rebel carries the risk of being shot. Acteal, Sabanilla, Nueva Esperanza, Tila, Agua Blanca, and San Geronimo Tulija are village communities that bear the marks of brutal massacre. But Mexico is only one example. On 10 November 1995, the Nigerian government executed the writer Ken Saro-Wiwa and eight others for agitating against the environmental ruin perpetuated by Shell.

Perhaps one can venture to say that the first phase of the anti-globalization agitation took place between 1994 – when the EZLN (Zapatista Army of National Liberation) opposed the implementation of the North American Free Trade Agreement on the very day that the accord was to be implemented, thereby declaring their sovereignty – and 2002, which was marked by protests against the World Economic Forum in New York City. The search for an alternative world model such as that initiated by the Zapatistas or the resistance of Chinese students in Tiananmen Square may spearhead global protest vigorous enough to dislodge globalization. The resistance of the Zapatistas keeps alive the hope that the masses will not remain silent for long. The end of the Vietnam war or the downfall of apartheid in Africa, as political events of the post-decolonization era, bear testimony to the power of the masses.

In Bolivia too, the water wars led to the formation of a group called *La Coordinadora* that, in effect, brought the functioning of the entire city to a halt. As with the Argentinian *piqueteros* in the 1990s who had blocked roads to register their protest against neoliberal reforms, the city's population appeared on the streets; the people went on general strike and roads, airports, places of work and offices were forcibly blocked. When the government did not relent, people refused to pay their bills to Bechtel. What followed was a clash in the market place between the two forces – the government and the people – resulting in a general rollback on the water rates, although the celebrations did not last long as the dictator president, Hugo Banzer, declared martial law, imprisoned *Coordinadora* leaders and imposed a curfew in the city in service to the multinational giant. It was only when thousands of activists all over the world, contacted electronically, began to unite and pressure Bechtel to leave the country that the policy to privatize water was reversed.

These struggles, which are often local, informal and unorganized, are not only anti-global in nature but also anarchical, that is, 'less about seizing state power than about exposing, delegitimizing, and dismantling mechanisms of rule while winning ever-larger spaces of autonomy from it' (Graeber 2003: 331). Members of groups like Reclaim the Streets, Black Bloc, Direct Action Network or Tuti Bianci are constituted of steel workers and Mohawk warriors, students and environmentalists, and people who tear down fences and walls to enact 'the single most powerful moment in the movement's history' (Graeber 2003: 328). The resistance to the construction of large dams such as the Sardar Sarovar Project, which proposes to build 3,166 dams on the river Narmada in Gujarat in India, is an initiative of the common people. Such massive projects displace thousands of villagers who sometimes wait a lifetime for the construction of new settlements. Bargi, the very first dam to be built on the Narmada, not only submerged more land than it irrigated, but also displaced 114,000 people, most of whom are still awaiting rehabilitation. In the Piparvati Resettlement Site, people have been waiting 20 years for the allotment of land. If they are allotted new dwellings at all, as in Mokhdi, another site, they face the prospect of acute shortage of fodder and water, and a breakdown of kinship ties as a result of being resettled in far-flung pockets of the state (Roy 2004: 3–9; 1999). The brunt, as usual, is borne by the tribals who are doomed to drown at the stroke of a bureaucratic pen. The initiatives of the Narmada Bachao Andolan (NBA or Save Narmada Movement) – spearheaded by Medha Patkar and later on, to a limited extent, by

Arundhati Roy – have met with a measure of success as the World Bank was forced to discontinue further funds for the project. The World Commission on Dams was also set up which aims to take note of the ill-effects of such enormous projects (Raina 2004: 10). Such acts of resistance and protest are outlets for outrage as well as 'windows – not only into another way to live, disengaged from the state, but also into a new politics of engagement' (Klein 2001).

Any discussion on global resistance movements would be incomplete without considering gender issues, especially the Chipko agitation in the Garhwal area of the Himalayas in 1971, another amazing example of a confrontational stand, this time by women, which resulted in a ten-year ban on the felling of trees. It was owing to the way in which women prevented deforestation by clinging to trees that the movement is known as 'Chipko', which literally means 'sticking'.[20] This example of linking traditional 'feminine' concerns with politics shows how women have used their socially prescribed roles to act politically, and to explore the relationship between gendered identities and political activity.[21] All such acts of dissent and activism against infra-structural projects initiated under the aegis of resistance to corporate globalization should be included in the term 'postcolonial'.

Postcolonial studies, however, does raise the theoretical question of the degree of inequality characteristic of feminism in postcolonial contexts, which serves to diffuse political action among women. The intervention of national politics, race, ethnicity, class, religion, region, sexuality and language exacerbates the complexity of gender issues and makes it difficult to establish common cause between the various categories. Protest and resistance is often contained when feminism is branded as a westernized, upper-class and urban movement focused on countering the oppression of the elite woman while ignoring that of her traditional third-world counterpart. Further, feminists in the third world often find themselves outnumbered by groups of women wooed by the tradition–modernity debate where feminism is deemed to involve a selling-out to the west. While all this is cogently argued in postcolonial feminist texts, the issue of protest is nevertheless diluted by such theorizing. Keeping the nation in perspective, postcolonial studies underplays the significance of women's resistance by highlighting the ways in which nationalism, historiography and democracy are intrinsically gendered.[22] While overarching, holistic campaigns for change have been known to thwart gender demands, to say that 'women who are not empowered to organize during the struggle will not be empowered to organize after the struggle' (McClintock 1991:122) is to run the risk of deferring women's demands indefinitely.[23] The sublimation of the entire discourse of nationalism within the auspices of motherhood is another postcolonial commonplace, overwhelming and ghettoizing protest within the macropolitical, masculine discourse of nationalism which purportedly remains fixed on the symbology of motherhood, as though women who enter public life primarily play maternal roles. This suggests that women's participation in the national struggle can only result in dashed hopes and betrayed promises as the new national policies, acquiescing to global pressures, neglect their subjects.

Traditional gender roles need not always be seen as stultifying; they may, in fact, have room for effective politicization outside the overused rubric of nationalism. In order to enunciate their personal politics, not only should the question of the oppression of women be legitimately addressed in the study of formal politics, but women must also ask for a fundamental transformation of the very definition of the word 'political' so that many of the activities undertaken by them can be included. This may even accommodate a politicized dimension of motherhood, not as it has been ideologically essentialized, but as a form of empowerment (Sethi 2007: 18). This might be the only way by which women can surmount the problems relating to race, caste, class and language. Environmental feminism is an area where the exploitation of women by global intervention in agricultural practices can be explained by positing the idea of the equation of women and nature on the grounds that both have been marginalized by male violence.[24] A theory about the protection of nature predicated upon the rejection of a 'masculinist' science can resist, albeit theoretically, those market forces of globalization which dictate the kind of agriculture the third world should practice. Suffice it to say here that a recovery and resilience of indigenous societies is possible which might change the way in which we perceive the culture of imperialism.

III

Globalization, however, is not simply about the irrevocable processes of coming into modernity or the growth of the economy of primitive societies. It has become an incarnation of the pressures exerted by the west, and now the United States in particular, on third-world nation-states, thereby turning an economic-historical process into what we call neocolonialism or, more acceptably, neoliberalism. Neoliberalism in the United States is based on two principles: one, to proclaim affluence everywhere while making promises of economic equality; and second, the show of economic strength to make developing countries remit their loans by using the power of the World Bank and the International Monetary Fund.

The intrusion of the liberal global governance of US corporate giants into the third world is programmed by the creation of a hospitable economic environment germane to the production of goods by private industry. At least 54 Special Economic Zones have been created out of prime farm land in India for the likes of Nike, Ranbaxy, Wockhardt, Infosys and Brandix Apparels. This has recently led to massive protests and general strikes by non-governmental organizations, tribals and squatters. Although public pressure has resulted in limiting land acquisition to 5,000 hectares per project, against the earlier norms where land was acquired without limit, who can stop another farmer from selling his land adjacent to the 5,000 hectares enabling the industrialist to build a complete city? Similarly, in the agricultural sector, the US is a major player in a new generational 'war' whose arsenal includes mainly trade treaties and monopolies of production that are governed by the rules of competition dictated by the west (Shiva 2005). Globalization wars are far more damaging than combat warfare because the ambit and arena is vast: the entire world is the enemy which has to be vanquished (Shiva

2005: viii). When the World Trade Organization was formed in 1995, there was a surplus of treaties giving the US a complete monopoly over seed and food. The ownership of rights over seeds began in 1991 when the Dunkel Draft Text offered an agreement relating to the patenting of seeds and the liberalization of exports and imports. In this kind of war zone, the world's resources are threatened by 'food wars' among a small number of companies (Shiva 2005: ix). Cargill and Monsanto, armed with forms of genetic engineering, nano-technologies and intellectual property rights, have introduced new kinds of 'criminalization' of agriculture in which farmers are prevented from using part of their own harvest as seeds for the next crop, thus breaking with the traditional practice. Patented, hybrid and non-reproducible seeds have to be purchased each year, which poor farmers can ill-afford.[25] The coercive WTO policies relating to patenting have, to a great extent, been responsible for poverty and poverty-related deaths. By far the greatest abuse of the powers of globalization is biopiracy, the ownership of intellectual rights by superpowers of the products grown indigenously by those over whom monopoly is exercised. By making minor modifications, patents are procured by firms and universities who then obtain intellectual rights and claim royalties over the product. The Neem plant, turmeric and basmati rice have all been exploited by American, European and Japanese firms who have flagrantly obtained numerous patents, thereby usurping knowledges that were heretofore indigenous (Shiva 2005: 86–109). Much in the same way, the excursions of *The Body Shop* founder, Anita Roddick, into non-western societies to procure ingredients like the aloe vera plant, have served to fulfil both the needs of globalization and the 'longing for the exotic and ethnic Other' which is part of the postmodern commodification of cultures (Sardar 1998: 124).[26]

Several decades ago, in 1960s India, the much-touted Green Revolution ushered in the US-imposed industrial/chemical farming that proved to be an ecological disaster, resulting in the erosion of the topsoil and leading to a shortage of water, contamination of the soil, the neglect of small farmers and a greater susceptibility to pests.[27] Its consequences have, paradoxically, benefited the agrochemical industry, the factories producing agricultural equipment and machinery, the builders of dams, and the petrochemical companies. But despite the pressures of green imperialism, instances of activism are not so isolated: the Karnataka State Farmers' Association (KRRS), which now boasts of ten million members, started the 'Operation Cremate Monsanto' to check the workings of the US-based corporation and discontinue its 'unmilled, self-sterilizing corn' (Mertes 2003: 152). Extremely Gandhian in its activism, farmers lit a bonfire that consumed their genetically modified cotton crops. Few would know that Monsanto had created the deadly Agent Orange during the Vietnam War. Market regulations also result in the importation of agricultural products which are sold cheaper than local produce. Unable to compete with the low price of imported goods, thanks to the Agreement on Agriculture signed under the auspices of the WTO, farmers in many states in India regularly commit suicide by drinking pesticide.

What is distinctive about the Karnataka State Farmers' Association is its focus on local village culture. The farmers and peasants organize on the level of 'direct democracy' which ensures that their decisions are profitable for every member of the community since they are all involved in making choices (Notes 2003: 154). This model also gives the villages a degree of independence from the state and agribusinesses. The KRRS also follows Gandhi's principles of nonviolence, with the subtle difference that violence against non-living objects (such as fences and walls) is not considered a violation at all. Much like Gandhi's critique of industrial society, the policies of the KRRS are based on maintaining ecological balance through traditional agricultural practices, the conservation of groundwater by removing eucalyptus trees, the use of traditional varieties of seed to support biodiversity and local food needs, and the use of traditional medicines so as to thwart an overdependence on rich pharmaceutical companies. What the KRRS practices is a sort of anti-globalization policy, the success of which could reduce food insecurity and introduce resilience into a degenerating ecosystem. This explains the opposition to GATT, the storming of the Cargill office in Bangalore in 1992, the indignation at the opening of the fast food chain Kentucky Fried Chicken in India in 1995, the protests against the Miss World pageant held in Bangalore in 1996, and so on. Farmers and peasants from the KRRS have gone as far as travelling to the WTO headquarters in Geneva in 1999 on a chartered Russian plane, to register their protest against trade liberalization and to denounce the seed hegemony of Cargill and the officious high-handedness of NATO in Brussels.[28]

The logic of the farmers is hard to ignore. In London, for instance, representatives of the Indian farmers union sit face to face with the public-relations managers of Life Science industries, who consider genetically modified crops to be the only way of keeping the southern poor from going hungry – whereupon the question is raised by the Secretary General of the Bharat Kisan Union (Indian Farmers' Union):

> Perhaps you believe that India needs genetically engineered seeds, or there will be famine? ... India has a surplus of food, and we have a problem of storage, not of shortage... This surplus is largely due to the production of small-scale peasant farmers. Even without genetically engineered seeds, we have surplus. So you can imagine our astonishment to hear from your report that we need genetically engineered food to feed ourselves. (Cited in Notes 2003: 167)

The proposal to grow GM crops is accompanied by the recommendations of the WTO to practice monocultural farming that includes floriculture, aquaculture and meat. Since the success or failure of harvest in the developing world depends on the vagaries of nature, the limitations imposed on growing only one or two types of crops poses the enormous risk of depleting local economies rather than improving the financial health of the farmers. Monocultures are responsible for draining the soil of particular kinds of nutrients; in forestry, the promotion of the growth of one species will undoubtedly have ramifications for plants and animals that require biodiversity in the ecosystem for their existence. In agriculture, particularly, a division between policies relating to goods in general and those relating to agriculture must be maintained (Amin 2004: 226–7). If agriculture, in which more than half the human race is involved, were made to follow agreements that the WTO has mandated, most of the farmers of the world would either starve or remain unabsorbed by industry even as they move to urban areas.

Such are the moments at which the nation-state must step in, as 'the only concrete terrain and framework for political struggle' (Jameson 2000: 65), with its food securities and safety nets to prevent the mafia-like control over agricultural policy that is widening the divide between market forces and the peasants.[29] In order to prevent liberalization-induced impoverishment, nation-states have to resist 'global governance without global government' (Stiglitz 2004: 204), refusing the dictates of elite countries and the lure of big corporates. Ways should be devised by which protection measures, quota systems and subsidies can co-exist with market liberalization and development. One cannot completely discount the appetite to accelerate productivity simply because the state is overwhelmed by the compulsions of capitalism or because a majority of farmers in the south are unable to keep pace with agricultural policies fashioned by the north. Globalization will not be resisted to the point of underdevelopment. Although globalization creates inequalities among people and perpetuates differences, trade has its uncontested benefits too.[30]

A greater interaction between the north and the south would undoubtedly assist third-world farmers and indigenous groups, sensitizing the north towards the crises of ecology and of capital affecting the south. Unilateral policies governing globalization should not be dictated by elite countries or be led by corporations, but should be need-based. In other words, there would have to be a 'new internationalism with a global vision' in which the two movements – globalization from above and globalization from below – would be enacted simultaneously (Brecher 2003: 203). While it is very possible that the former will overpower the latter, there is hope that a better equilibrium between the two can be established as a check to market fundamentalism.[31]

As a counter to the processes of neoliberalism, meetings of the World Social Forum (WSF) are held annually to explore the ideal of an alternative world. The alternative world model, a sort of 'international citizenship' which aims at 'winning back the knowledge that leads to the recovery of power' (Jennar 2004: 290), offers the potential of making people conscious of the agendas of the Bretton Woods institutions (WTO, World Bank, IMF) which follow the dictates of the prosperous G8 nations.[32] Like the WSF, Oxfam International has enumerated modes of operations to combat the evils of neoliberalism and made suggestions to improve market conditions for poor countries so that they are neither coerced into removing subsidies for their agricultural produce nor impelled to accept the export dumping of rich countries. It is recommended that there should be a radical overhauling of IMF and World Bank programmes so that poor countries are not obliged to open their markets. Oxfam has also promoted ideas of new intellectual property rights, diversification of goods and the democratization of the WTO to allow more participation by the poor countries in decision making and evolving new national guidelines in relation to public works, education and welfare (Mestrum 2004: 191–2).

But in spite of such prescriptions and directives, there is seldom any radical denunciation of poverty or a demand for a different way of life. The 'alternative world movement' may profess to be 'reformist', but 'does not declare that it is against capitalism ... [since] democracy, human rights and the United Nations constitute part of the gains from liberalism' (Mestrum 2004: 89). Oxfam's adjudication and suggestions imply that the WTO proposals have been used to reduce disparities but, contrary to expectation, Oxfam permits rightful trade with one hand and pulls down democracy with the other. It both endorses democratic rights and free will as accompaniments to trade, yet derides democracy and sovereignty as obstacles to it. Trade is promoted but with scant regard for the degeneration of ecosystems and the fundamental right of people to live in a clean and healthy environment. Oxfam, which began as an organization to address food shortages and famine, fails to give reasons why the increase in food grain export leads to a decline in food output per head locally. It has thus been rapped on the knuckles by critics like Vandana Shiva who demonstrate that the benefits of free trade have always been reaped by the rich rather than the poor and that exports from the south to the north only serve to reduce agricultural products for home consumption (Shiva 2002: n.p.).

Non-Governmental Organizations set up for public redress become agents of neoliberal capitalism enfeebling the once powerful nation-states. The neoliberal capitalist model of globalization, with the US at its helm, prevents governments from pursuing public interest schemes. The dissatisfaction with the existing handiwork of the superpowers and the vulnerabilities of the state, the failed promises of non-governmental organizations, and the hope for the emergence of an alternative world have, as yet, not been able to throw up solutions for the variety of developing countries that exist in different relationships with centres of power. Brecher poses a succession of questions in this regard:

> How should globalization from below envision the process of change? Is it like a series of national reforms? A series of national revolutions? A world revolution? The taking over of corporations by those they affect? The formation of a democratic world government? Or something unlike any of these? (Brecher 2003: 209)

While few would claim to know the answers to these questions, it is at least clear that there has to be coordination between the alternative movements themselves to initiate joint action among pressure groups. In the absence of such management skills, there is bound to be fragmentation of intent and extreme isolation as each group struggles in its individual pocket. The impoverished south has to look for 'alliances among the women's movement, the fish workers' movement, the farmers' movement, the tribal and indigenous peoples' movement' so that those who 'live on the natural-resource-base' by dint of their own labour can keep privation at bay (Patkar, cited in Notes 2003: 296–7). Although a 'lilliput strategy', globalization from below links people from different nationalities with diverse agendas as well as people working with grassroots groups so that they can defend themselves against big businesses, corporations and the international financial institutions (Brecher 2003: 204).[33]

The concerns that have been outlined here are real (rather than hyperreal) issues in the lives of marginalized communities of the postcolonial world. The inability to account for neocolonialism and the inadequacy in relating theory to actual resistance are the shortcomings of postcolonial analyses.[34] Among the factors that have led to the stagnation of postcolonial studies is its disinheritance of accounts of grassroots struggles constituting 'postcolonial practice', primarily as a result of its neglect of the nation-state. Even though theories of globalization are located in the decline of the nation-state, there is still plenty of evidence of 'national' narratives that can resist, or at least subvert, the dark side of globalization. In the many examples cited here, resistance is not necessarily conducted through the nation-state, as Marxists suggest, but regardless of the nation-state or in actual defiance of it. The women who clung to trees and prevented deforestation, the Zapatistas who fought against *neoliberalismo* for their survival, the members of the *Coordinadora* with their water wars in Bolivia, the protesting tribals on the banks of the river Narmada who were evicted by the construction of big dams, or even the Maoist 'terrorists' of Chhattisgarh in central India, who are presently militating against the mining of their forest land as hundreds of Memoranda of Understanding amounting to billions of dollars are being signed with transnational corporations – each in their limited ways are engaged in civil insurgency against their own state for speaking the language of global capital, and are endeavouring to reclaim their nation.[35] They are hardly like the 'legendary subalterns of colonial culture' because 'when they speak, they sometimes speak a language that is alien to their liberal sympathizers or the postcolonial émigré elite' (Gikandi 2001: 644). These are not groups of people who desire to live in a chimera or a virtual world which amplifies with their distance from the metropolitan centres, as Appadurai suggests (Appadurai 2000: 1809). On the contrary, these are people who want stable lives even though migration and exile, consciously or otherwise, form part of their lived experience. Whether they move to Dubai or Mumbai, they do so not with a throbbing need to embrace hybridity but with a desire to attain prosperity, just like Gikandi's narrative of two unfortunate boys from Guinea whose bodies were asphyxiated in a plane to Brussels as they tried to cross illegally into Europe in the hope of finding joy and prosperity (Gikandi 2001: 630).[36] Those who form part of the labour and refugee diaspora, unlike the tourist diaspora, move in search of better means of survival and possible wealth not available in the land of their birth. Yes, they do have dreams and fantasies but these cannot be contained within alterity and difference; rather, the imagined worlds of the underprivileged accentuate the insurmountable gap between first-world privilege and third-world poverty.

4

THE UNITED STATES AND POSTCOLONIALISM

Even as the United States was assuming the mantle of a global superpower, Edward Said had traced the correspondence of American neocolonialism to both its orientalist tendencies in the past and the imperial policies of the nineteenth-century colonizers – Britain, Spain, France and Portugal. The final chapters of Said's *Orientalism* and *Culture and Imperialism* are concerned with the consolidation of US hegemony after the Second World War. The issue of the US as a global power is not unrelated to its cultural history and the American Studies curriculum taught in its universities. But, lately, US hegemony is being imposed through new curricula that are advancing a global terminology, and the importation of faculty/academic celebrities from the field of postcolonialism. Postcolonialism seems to be taking a new trajectory here in that we find postcolonial theory and literatures being taught in most universities in the US today. It thus becomes important to investigate the inclusion of the United States into postcolonial studies.

Postcolonial studies and the US have a deep and binding connection – the very settling of the people of Europe in a new continent since 1492, the extermination of the inhabitants of the First Nations, and the transportation of millions of slaves over the Atlantic, are themselves postcolonial concerns. Yet postcolonial studies has not adapted easily to American climes in the way that conditions in Asia, Africa and Latin America have made its existence possible. Actual political struggles for decolonization in these areas might be among the reasons for the adaptability of postcolonial studies, an experience and ideology missing in the

United States. And although questions of race, genocide, multi-culturalism and ethnic identity abound here, its academy has not been able to use postcolonial paradigms perceptively to examine American Studies.

While addressing the politics of location of the term 'postcolonial', Ella Shohat has questioned why the United States should be labelled 'postcolonial' even though it had been 'colonized', notionally at any rate, by the British until the American War of Independence in 1776 (Shohat 1992: 102). To go a stage further and explore the reverse of this proposition – how the US is the contemporary perpetrator of the ancient colonialism model, since there is nothing 'postcolonial' about its behaviour – is also an issue I will be taking up in what follows. At the time when manifestoes of decolonization were being written by Fanon, Césaire and others who questioned western representations, the master-narratives of the United States were chauvinistically expressing the necessity of imperialism to the formation of its culture.

While these are ongoing debates, they also raise questions as to whether it is possible any longer to keep the US separate from postcolonial studies especially in view of 1) transnational capitalism and 2) the presence of ethnic minorities in the US who are victims of cultural anxiety placed as they are both within and without American identity. More than ever, it is becoming increasingly important to reconsider the concept of postcolonialism and rethink directions for postcolonial studies, especially after 9/11, which has once more consolidated the coalition forces and the 'civilizational' notion of western values. There is a need also to discuss the intersection of postcolonialism and American Studies to show that US cultural history has always been a contested terrain of imperial and colonial experiences.

I

What is known as American Studies mainly includes the examination and analysis of the national culture of the United States, its history and literature, within which the focus has gradually moved onto issues of race, ethnicity and empire. For most American academic institutions, what is called 'postcolonial' tends to include areas supposedly outside American concerns, such as South Asia, the Middle East, East Asia and Africa (Schwarz 2000: 8). Very often, especially in the departments of English, it is seen as an 'add on' to the ethnic studies curriculum – the study of its native American, African-American, Asian-American, and Latin and Hispanic populations – a simple extension of its existing studies on multiethnic literatures of the US to those of the world.

For its part, postcolonial studies has also fashioned its own now well-established canon which does not allow it to study American culture in a favourable way (King 2000: 3), the reason being that America has hardly ever been associated with the history of colonialism. Europe, especially Britain, and its colonies, have been the focus of postcolonial studies to such an extent that America's only mark in this area has been its own 'independence' from Britain. Richard King points out that it is professionally believed that colonialism has never been part of US history and that US identities and cultural formations were unaffected by imperialist policy in any manner whatsoever (King 2000: 3). Likewise, some critics have shown impatience more than wariness of its new imperial tendencies when discussing the inclusion of the US in contemporary postcolonial studies.[1] While the popularization of ethnic studies in the US academic circuit owes its 'internationalism', in some measure, to the gloss acquired from the proliferation of postcolonialism in the wider world, postcolonial studies did not exhibit any marked proclivity to examine ethnic studies, or indeed American culture, at least not until the 1980s. The reason, primarily, was the anxiety relating to the potential loss of political energy and momentum if postcolonialism was to identify with ethnic or race matters. But with the arrival of postcolonial theorists in the United States, not only did postcolonialism begin to take on innumerable connotations, its formal appearance in the US also became the harbinger of its eventual entrenchment. As postcolonial studies becomes increasingly linked with immigration, race and ethnicity in the US, and with a host of other initiatives all over the world, it runs the risk of playing into the hands of a liberal multiculturalism that obfuscates even the significance of 'race' and becomes a 'new universalism of the sort it was established to critique' (Sharpe 2000b: 123).

Yet one of the earliest books on postcolonial studies, *The Empire Writes Back*, claims that the United States was 'the first post-colonial society to develop a "national" literature' and further that the experience of the US as it consolidated power has been 'paradigmatic for post-colonial literatures everywhere' (Ashcroft et al. 1989: 16, 2). The race to include the literature of the United States under the aegis of postcolonialism may have been spurred by this statement, although the three authors do not elaborate any further. *The Empire Writes Back* loses a lot in terms of the contemporary implications of colonialism by defining the 'postcolonial' in vague, loose terms: postcolonial 'cover[s] all the culture affected by the imperial process from the moment of colonization to the present day' (Ashcroft et al. 1989: 2). The definition given by Ashcroft and others veers towards a culturalist interpretation of postcolonialism, sacrificing the material circumstances and capitalist motives inherent in the entire enterprise of colonialism from the moment of the exploration of colonies to their independence and current subjugation under new forms of economic control.[2] The latter is especially relevant when we configure the role of the US in the postcolonial climate.

As far as the United States is concerned, the convention of dominating its indigenous communities cannot be seen as distinct from that of colonization in the rest of the world, even though neither African-Americans nor American-Indians could stand in for the Caliban figure (Schueller and Watts 2003: 13).[3] One uncomfortable 'postcolonial' truth which America's white settler population has in common with Canada and Australia, countries that were declared dominions of Britain, is the extermination or complete marginalization of native populations by the early discoverers and first settlers. The foundation of American experience is a reminder 'that this nation owes its very existence to colonialism, and that along with settlers and immigrants there have always been conquered Indians and black slaves, and later defeated Mexicans – that is, colonial subjects – on national soil'

(Blauner 2001: 46). So what does 'postcolonialism' mean for the United States? Frankenberg and Mani offer an extended description of this complex relationship:

> Here, the term 'postcolonial' sticks in our throats. White settler colony, multiracial society. Colonization of Native Americans, Africans imported as slaves, Mexicans incorporated by a border moving south, Asians imported and migrating to labor, white Europeans migrating to labor. US imperialist foreign policy brings new immigrants who are 'here because the US was/ is there', among them central Americans, Koreans, Filipinos, Vietnamese and Cambodians. The particular relation of past territorial domination and current racial composition that is discernible in Britain, and which lends a particular meaning to the term 'postcolonial', does not, we feel, obtain here. (Frankenberg and Mani 2000: 1847)

One of the reasons why the US appears to be an aberrant colony is its early colonial status and early independence as compared with the other colonies of Britain, not to speak of its later advent into neocolonialism (Stratton 2000: 61). It is far more appropriate to associate the US with the position of a colonizer than with the colonized owing not just to its past history but also to the presence of its economically marginalized minorities: despite the rhetoric of the 'melting pot' theory, 'the ghettos, barrios, internment camps, and reservations [continue to be] the "internal colonies" of the United States' (Sharpe 2000a: 105). 'Racism' rather than 'postcolonialism' is still the more appropriate term in the context of the United States.[4] But since the issue of the rights of minorities emerged from political movements related to decolonization in the third world – whereby the disenfranchisement of blacks, native Americans, Asian-Americans, Mexicans and others became associated with forms of colonialism – studies in the US have sought a postcolonial connection. However, 'internal colonialism' can neither be conflated with the histories of colonialism nor cover the contingencies of recent immigrants who are pursuing their own American experience by desiring, more often than not, to assimilate into American culture. Frankenberg and Mani use the term 'post-Civil Rights' as an alternative to describe recent American history (Frankenberg and Mani 2000:

1847). Nevertheless, this term has its own set of problems given its implication of 'post-racist', which would not be a fair description of contemporary American society. Both 'posts' here suggest an unfinished business – as does postcolonialism – and not the culmination of a process (Frankenberg and Mani 2000: 1848). And because there is something inconclusive about it, native Americans, blacks, migrants and ethnic minorities have not shown great alacrity in welcoming it.

Contrary to misgivings on both sides, there is an entire corpus of academics who attempt to discover a connection between postcolonialism and the US, despite admitting to an 'uneasiness' and 'awkwardness' (King 2000: 9). Many collections of essays, including King's *Postcolonial America*, explore 'national narratives, transnational formations, and local elaborations of postcoloniality in American culture' (King 2000: 11). Henry Schwarz's introductory essay in *A Companion to Postcolonial Studies* argues against bypassing the role of the US altogether, emphasizing how the 'productive potential' of this discipline opens up a 'materially grounded postcolonial studies' which allows an understanding of 'ethnicity in the Americas', an inclusion that will help problematize the complexity of power relations in the world (Schwarz 2000: 6). 'Postcoloniality', from this formulation, would enable a more equitable basis of knowledge production (Schwarz 2000: 7). The emphasis, as one can see, is upon the ethnic and the local, yet the repercussions are worldwide. In other words, here we find a focus on American localism that would go on to change the orientation, or perhaps the foundation, of a discipline seen as central to the contemporary identities of formerly colonized countries. Such contributions to postcolonial studies work for only a local readership because they include the multiethnic people of the United States who are marginalized in quite other ways. Schwarz even hijacks Said's *Orientalism* as 'a profoundly American book' (Schwarz 2000: 11). This would be a different postcolonial studies, one would surmise, that rhymes with ethnic studies. In fact, Amritjit Singh and Peter Schmidt's book, *Postcolonial Theory and the United States*, attempts to mediate between postcolonialism and ethnicity by invoking phrases like 'our shared human histories' and 'our growing global interdependence' (Singh and Schmidt 2000: viii) to produce a veritable 'American Studies'.

One reason for the possibility of the inclusion of the US into postcolonial studies is the instability of the term 'postcolonial'. Its original links with postmodernism divert attention from issues of being and belonging that should be central to studies about postcolonialism. Hardt and Negri's *Empire* changed the equation somewhat by arguing that Empire was imbued with postmodern tendencies and that it was less centred at one point or vested in one power. The adjectival blooming of terminology such as 'postcoloniality' or 'postcolonial cultures' further tends to reduce the political accountability of the term and extends the threshold for postcolonial studies to embrace other cultures that are characterized by marginality. Thus delineated, postcolonial studies begins to resemble a 'cultural' outfit that is 'not limited to regions, but rather travel[s] between various locations simultaneously' (Schwarz 2000: 16). Within such frameworks, many contributors to these anthologies have chosen to examine the institutional emergence of postcolonial studies in the US. Its rise and growth here might also be linked to its suitability as the official vehicle of dissent for the very cultures that are embroiled in colonialism across the world. Protesting voices are often commissioned by the offices of dominating cultures as a gesture towards their anti-hegemonic tendencies.

There are two reasons why the thesis of postcoloniality in the United States championed in recent anthologies (the three mentioned above all appeared in the year 2000) cannot hold good. The first of these has to do with the case of what is called American 'exceptionalism': the view that 'America' is different from any other country, particularly Britain, and that its history was written on a clean slate after the earliest white settlers had moved to North America. This may be America's means of severing connections with the 'mother country', as did scores of countries in Asia and Africa after decolonization. As Schwarz puts it:

> The fundamental beliefs in justice, democracy, and equal opportunity that are said to characterize the American Revolution (1776), the Civil War

> (1860–5), and today color America's relation with the rest of the world are deeply enshrined in this American mythology and are considered uniquely ('exceptional') American values. (Schwarz 2000: 9)

An average American is raised in the climate of these values upheld by the belief in America's 'manifest destiny'. In order to become 'typically' American, all migrants have to be American in every way by sacrificing cultural difference. The origin of American exceptionalism lies in two significant doctrines – George Washington's Farewell Address of 1796 and the 1823 Monroe Doctrine. The former advocates a disconnection from Europe and the latter warns Europe against messing with its erstwhile colonies. John Winthrop perhaps best summed up the theme of American separatism when he said: 'We shall be as a city upon a hill, the eyes of all people upon us' (cited in Rowe 2000b: 3) The 'national meta-narrative' of America is constructed out of phrases such as these.

Thus it is that syllabi taught in US universities still focus on the texts that emphasize American exclusivity: R. W. B. Lewis's *American Adam* (1955), Perry Miller's *Errand into the Wilderness* (1956) and *Nature's Nation* (1963)[5] end up aiding and abetting American exceptionalism despite the contrary signs of European immigration, the extermination or marginalization of the Indian population and their specific histories, and the expansion of the United States particularly through the usurpation of Mexican lands. Exceptionalism lies in derecognizing the role of conquest, war and exploitation in achieving economic expansion so that imperialism and complete innocence can exist hand in hand to create, shall we say, a willing suspension of disbelief or, as Pease puts it, 'structures of denial' (Pease 2000: 204). US exceptionalism is something of an oxymoron because it includes the disavowal of imperialism even as the latter is central to its global power and is consciously exercised.[6] Who can deny the enslavement of the blacks and the internal colonialism of antebellum America, or the colonial status of Central and Latin America, East Asia, the Philippines and the Caribbean, and most recently Iraq? Yet this 'indispensable nation', as Madeleine Albright calls it (Albright

1998), has always violated human rights in many parts of the world and then offered a moral legitimacy for these exceptions by evoking a rhetoric of self-styled names – 'redeemer nation', 'nation of nations', 'leader of the free world', 'conqueror of the world's markets', and so on (Pease 2000: 205). The early Puritan fathers were no strangers to this hypermasculine narrative of the US when they displaced the native Indians on the basis of saving their souls. This view of American disavowal has parallels with Said's contrapuntal reading in *Culture and Imperialism*, though to a much milder degree, of the nineteenth-century English novel, into which the factuality of British colonialism seeps in imperceptibly, almost unknowingly. The inhabitants of Austen's Mansfield Park, Lord Bertram's country house, can enjoy their English tea while, unknown to them, thousands of miles away in Antigua, Bertram's slaves are 'tending his colonial garden' (Said 1993: 102, 107). The American psyche, in allied ways, desists from acknowledging imperialism:

> [S]o influential has been the discourse insisting on American specialness, altruism, and opportunity that 'imperialism' as a word or ideology has turned up only rarely and recently in accounts of the United States culture, politics, history. But the connection between imperial politics and culture is astonishingly direct. (Said 1993: 7)

Seen in such a light, there is little difference between British and American imperialisms, both of which are nourished by cultural myths of the nation. The American folklore validating imperialism contains a cultural repertoire which is constantly improvised to suit political expediency.[7] Aggressive phrases and rhetoric about the 'New World Order' are employed to invoke the myth of the Promised Land. One of the governing metaphors associated with current American hegemony is that of the apocalypse, within which society collapses into a chaos ruled by the beast of the apocalypse until the final restoration of order. Those who survive the catastrophe enter the promised land (Stratton 2000: 22). Cult American films have contributed enormously to establishing the image of the apocalypse and the subsequent attainment of the promised land in securing American identity. The impact of *Star Wars*, which best exemplifies the US–USSR Cold War mythology (Stratton 2000: 32), and the series of *Rambo* films that painstakingly reconstruct American supremacy despite the fiasco of the Vietnam war, cannot be overestimated. In similar spirit, *Casablanca* is nothing but a boost to the notion of the 'American century', as Henry Luce, editor of *Life* magazine, once called the twentieth century, even though it was shot among native Moroccans (Edwards 2003: 74–81). Postcolonial America, like postcolonial Britain which re-enacts nostalgia for the Raj by replaying films by David Lean and Merchant-Ivory on the BBC, has largely sustained its postcolonial identity by deliberately reconstructing it through film. *Apocalypse Now*, in this scenario, becomes the paradigm of the perfect 'postcolonial' film, particularly since it is modelled on *Heart of Darkness*, Conrad's eulogy to colonialism. Though it asserts ultimate US hegemony it also 'articulates the renewed uncertainty of the United States as a settler society' that has to be constantly fed to nourish its sense of identity, which can be fulfilled only with the attainment of the promised land (Stratton 2000: 37, 38–42). The new dawn of US imperialism, hailed aggressively by Niall Fergusson more recently in support of the ideology of Pax Americana, follows the essence of American exceptionalism (Fergusson 2001).

The contradictory thesis of national identity couched in the acknowledgement of America's great tolerance for national and ethnic diversity marks the entry of postcolonial studies into the university. Yet postcolonial specialists were not comfortable with US hegemony on the one hand and the seemingly pluralistic bearings of Pax Americana on the other. The spirit of questioning came from scores of scholars from other countries who chose to settle in the US for professional reasons. The 1960s and 1970s marked the opening up of US immigration policy with regard to professionals from abroad. Many of these intellectuals became pioneers in their fields and their influence on American thinking was enormous. Said's *Orientalism* is a case in point. The book could be used to review the new colonialism of the US and its attitude towards its ethnic minorities. Said's critique of French and British orientalisms became a means to provoke the conscience of even the most indifferent American scholar, especially in relation to the creation of oriental stereotypes existing in the western world. The 'free world' initiatives promoted by the US could now be seen as strategies of neocolonial rule and prevent scholars from posting the 'post' before the 'colonial'.

Notwithstanding the in-built critique of its own hegemonic practices, the US university system dexterously transforms its ideology of 'exceptionalism' into a symptom of postcoloniality, reinventing the romance of America's uniqueness as a significant contribution to its growth as a nation. The idea of cultural nationalism, constituted as a mythic identity related to the past, is advanced by the term 'America', in contrast to the political organism signalling independence implied by the phrase 'United States'.[8] The former is part of the 'postcolonial imaginary' while the latter is analogous to the nation-state that emerged as a neocolonial power; the former keeps the nation alive while the latter widens the hegemony of globalization.[9] Together the two – 'America' and the 'United States' – bear testimony to a postcolonial quest concerned with the crisis of identity of a displaced people. To aggressively promote its sense of being a nation-state, some of the most effective ways of downscaling heterogeneity employed in what is still the most powerful channel of protest – the university – include syllabi changes, marginalization of dissenting faculty members, selective funding for projects, and so on. Thus, much university research is done 'within the TNC space, inside the insider's globe' by 'current postcolonial TNC intellectuals': 'the old "self" and the old "other" are now comfortable with each other, and together they ignore the new "other"' (Miyoshi 1997: 61). Themes of hybridity and ambivalence in academia permit intellectuals to maintain and support an either/or politics. But outside the university, America uses its military might and the rhetoric of good versus evil. In terms of US politics, past and present, it might be more correct to contest the term 'postcolonial' in relation to the rise of the US as a neocolonial power and the control it exercises over global capitalism in the world than with reference to its history of exceptionalism.

II

The second reason for the error in labelling the US as 'postcolonial' lies in its engagement with neocolonialism, in which global hegemony plays a big part. By the end of the Second World War, the ill effects of the Depression in the US had been left behind, and even Britain had begun to acknowledge the dominance of the United States. Yet a return to a peace-time economy would have resulted in large-scale unemployment and affected the goods industry, thereby recreating the conditions that had existed in the 1930s. To ward off the dangers of a reversal in the economy, President Truman decided to fight 'communism' in Greece and Turkey in 1947. This coincided with the initiation of the Marshall Plan to build a powerful economy based on the principles of capitalism. The focus had to shift from production to finance if the US was to become a capitalist superpower.

Deindustrialization moved the US economy towards finance capital and at the same time severely decimated the power of the proletariat. The consequences were low wages, poor living and health conditions, unemployment, but also, of course, accelerated consumerism. Decades later, President Reagan's aggression towards trade unionism was evident in his relentless attitude towards the Professional Air Traffic Controllers Organization. The miners' strike in Britain was also frustrated for similar motives. So drastically did the US economy move into finance capitalism that by the time Bill Clinton moved into office he was to find a well-oiled machine run according to the so-called 'Washington consensus' that made sure the US retained its hegemonic position. The Bush administration differed greatly from Clinton's. In contrast to the latter's economic policies of globalization, the Bush government overtly deployed its military power. Where Clinton trod softly, went along as far as possible with multiculturalism and difference, and based decision-making on multilateral policies, Bush favoured the 'hard as nails' approach. But no matter what the differences between administrations, the imperial strides made by the US have been unambiguous and firm. Ever since the 1960s, US invasions in Latin America and South-East Asia have established its uncontested hegemony. In Haiti, for example, the most arable lands are used for the cultivation of coffee, sugar and cacao exacted by the US.[10] Though imperialism has been arrested by national struggles around the world, American unilateralism in world politics re-establishes its foothold as the legitimate corollary of its advancement. The unceasing and brutal economic policies generated by the US, the growing unemployment resulting from unfettered trade and market fundamentalism, the insidious military support given to Pakistan and earlier to Iraq, and the 'talibanization' of countries such as Afghanistan deflates the trust and confidence reposed in the 'new world order'. The demise of imperialism remains a distant dream.

Even before 9/11, Bush's unilateral policies rejected international treaties such as those seeking to try war criminals in special courts, to ensure the management of greenhouse gases, or, most importantly, to limit antiballistic missiles. The 'doctrine of preventive war', which allows the US to arbitrate between good and evil and tame 'uncivilized' nations, goes against all international agreements of the past. It permits the United States alone to have unchallenged power in the new world. It would not be incorrect to say that the US military primarily exists to aid the US economy. Hence, it was profitable to prolong the Cold War by equating Communist countries with terrorist regimes and thereby increase the defence budget. Accordingly, the Pentagon becomes 'the US equivalent of Japan's Ministry of International Trade and Industry; it plans and executes a centrally organized economic policy [which makes it] accurate to say that national security questions [are] essentially economic in nature' (Miyoshi 2000: 1872). True enough, America's defence-related transnational corporations are enormous and among the wealthiest: General Motors, General Electric, DuPont, Dow Chemical and so on. The defence of the country, once primary to the security and permanence of a nation-state, now exists only to support its economy.

The events of 9/11 allowed George Bush to raise the decoy of Saddam Hussein as an incarnation of evil, with the intention of using the US war machine to annihilate it and thereby quell unrest and insecurity in American civil society as well as lend support to the economic interests of its large corporations.[11] To paraphrase a familiar adage: 'If there were no enemy, it would be necessary to invent one.' Much before 9/11, Bush's circle of advisors – Rumsfeld, Wolfowitz, Armitage, Perle and others – had declared how imperative it was for the US to redraw the map of the Middle East by military intervention in order to safeguard its interests in Iraqi oil. Iraq, in fact, is a small part of a grand design; the real 'postcolonial' interest of the US lies in controlling the Middle East: 'whoever controls the Middle East controls the global oil spigot and whoever controls the global oil spigot can control the global economy, at least for the near future' (Harvey 2003: 19). By having a pro-US government in Iraq, it might be possible to effect political changes in Iran and Syria and perhaps even Saudi Arabia. It was during the Second World War that the US plotted ways of establishing control over the Middle East, as a means of establishing economic, military and political power over countries that held most of the oil resources in the world. Part of this venture involved the overthrow of the Mossadegh government in Iran and the installation of the Shah of Iran, Muhammad Reza Pehlavi, on the throne. The end of the dictatorial rule of the Shah in 1979, and the increase in the price of oil since 1973 by the OPEC countries, culminated in America's unstinting support to Iraq to increase its hostilities with Iran leading to a protracted eight-year war between the two countries. Iraq's invasion of Kuwait then created the perfect opportunity for America to send its forces to the Middle East.

More recently, bizarre attempts have been made to connect Saddam with the 9/11 events through Osama bin Laden, through myths about Iraq's arsenal of WMD and even by linking Saddam to the anthrax attacks in the United States. All for Oil. As Harvey writes humorously:

> And if all that failed, then Saddam had to go because he was a liar (an appellation that sticks to so many politicians that it quickly became a joke), ruthless (but then so [was] Sharon), reckless (not proven), or an incarnation

> of evil that had to be combated as if war in the Middle East was an episode in some long-running medieval morality play. (Harvey 2003: 11)

If the US is able to hold on to Iraq and also step into Iran, it can safely remain a global power as well as a military-industrial complex for the next five decades despite the depletion of its own oil reserves. As Hannah Arendt said in *The Origins of Totalitarianism*: 'A never-ending accumulation of property must be based on a never-ending accumulation of power ... The limitless process of capital accumulation needs the political structure of so "unlimited a Power" that it can protect growing property by constantly growing more powerful' (Arendt 1962: 143). In other words, power has to increase with the growth of capital, thus creating conditions for the existence of a hegemonic superpower. In the case of the US, it has become a 'rogue state' because in attempting to uphold its supremacy it has staged coups in Vietnam, Chile, Iran, Iraq, Guatemala, Brazil, Indonesia and several other countries, and even succeeded in having Saddam Hussein hanged for genocide through chemical warfare against the Kurds, the sort of crime the US itself has blatantly committed a number of times.[12] From attacking communism and promoting private property, this 'neocolonial bully' (O'Brien 2000: 71) has graduated to unleashing a 'war on terror' to protect its oil interests once it had accomplished the dismembering of the Soviet Union. Terror has indeed given greater powers to the US: 'America's entire war on terror is an exercise in imperialism. This may come as a shock to Americans, who don't like to think of their country as an empire. But what else can you call America's legions of soldiers, spooks and Special Forces straddling the globe?' (Ignatieff 2002: 1). What distinguishes early American imperialism from British colonialism is the former's ability to initiate hegemony by 'invitation' rather than coercion (Lundestad 1986: 263), although coercive means gradually became its dominant modus operandi. Nevertheless, US policies during Bush's presidency acquired popular support among the media; as Thomas Friedman wrote regarding US hostilities in Iraq: 'There is nothing illegitimate or immoral about the US being concerned that an evil, megalomaniacal dictator might acquire excessive influence over the natural resource that powers the world's industrial base' (Friedman 2003).

If the invasion of Iraq can be seen as an imperial endeavour to gain control over oil, what sort of plans does the US have for its future? Quite possibly, Iraq is to become 'a model for the rest of the Middle East' (Harvey 2003: 197), developed as it has been along the lines of a 'free society'. The Iraqi government is predictably weak, and given to cronyism, while Iraqi oil not only pays for the reconstruction of the country's own broken economy but helps to bolster the global economy. Possible future US forays into Iran and Syria may provide a boost to its economy and military that will subdue North Korea or any other power that chooses to cross swords with it. Further, if the US can tie up with Poland, Bulgaria and Turkey, it can be assuredly superior to every other power (China or the EU, for instance) for decades to come.[13]

But such self-aggrandizement and large ambitions are very likely to alienate the United States' closest ally, Britain, and also provoke Germany, France, Russia and China into a relationship of convenience. Spain and Italy, too, are likely to become strained with the US and give in to their own people's demands to pursue a different course. Much depends of course on more recent political changes in all these countries – in particular the possibility of new linkages between David Cameron in Britain and Democrat Barack Obama in the US – whereafter ideologies and alliances may alter over time. However, at present, in spite of the new administration in the US and repeated assertions that the Obama government will reverse Bush's foreign policy, its global imperial posture stands roughly as before. The US has neither reduced military spending nor sacrificed its military rhetoric.[14]

What is even more disturbing than the hegemonic designs of the US is its disposition to exhibit a marked anti-colonial stance in its social and cultural transactions with the world (see Rowe 2000a: 3–4). Quoting Van Alstyne, Rowe, in his study of the colonial nature of American policy since the eighteenth century, lists a series of descriptions that have been used by US foreign policy exponents to proclaim its lack of hegemonic intent: 'Monroe Doctrine', 'freedom of the seas', 'open door' and 'good neighbour policy' are some examples (Rowe 2000a: 4). So insistent has been the US oratory about anti-colonialism that it addresses European excesses in the colonial era as imperialist and its own ventures in North America as an exercise in 'national consolidation'. Again, its promises of egalitarianism and even-handedness to its many hyphenated groups, such as native Americans, African-Americans, Chinese-Americans and Latin-Americans among others, must be balanced against its drive towards self-promotion which underscores the ideology of eliminating minority cultures (Rowe 2000a: 5). Rowe contends that any nation with such a track record of prejudice against its domestic population is scarcely likely to have a clean register overseas: 'Virtually from the moment the original colonies defined themselves as a nation, there was an imperial project to restrict the meaning of the American by demonizing foreigners, in part by identifying them with the "savagery" ascribed to Native and African Americans' (Rowe 2000a: 7). Such has been the erratic narrative of the 'cosmopolitanism' of the United States.

III

Allow me to go back to the moment of postcolonialism. The year 1947 signalled the opening up of the colonial world, a release for South Asian nations from the long period of European eclipses and influences. Politically, the 1955 Bandung Conference marked their 'non-aligned' status which made clear that European hegemony in every form was over. In 1987, the United Nations recorded 160 states as having achieved their independence. With the end of the Cold War, several others were to join this newly 'empowered' group. At this juncture, postcolonialism zoomed into focus as a radical philosophy that promised not only to expose the ways and means by which territory and sensibility are colonized but also to show how knowledge itself is a form of colonialism[15] and that to study western scholarship, particularly English literature, would contribute to its growth. Postcolonialism sought to make accountable all forms of dominance and marginality, hegemony and oppression. In other words, postcolonial ideology stretched beyond colonial despotism to all kinds of structures of oppression existing not only in the postcolonial world but also in the west, being therefore 'not merely a theory of knowledge but a "theoretical practice", a transformation of knowledge from static disciplinary competence to activist intervention' (Schwarz 2000: 4). Thus, theory and activism, by this definition, were to be the hallmarks of postcolonialism.

This understanding of the origins of postcolonialism exposes the problem, stated at the outset, with recent collections of postcolonial writing in the United States. Many of these anthologies are preoccupied with twentieth-century concerns, prominent among them being the existence of the US as an empire with a mixed population espousing multiculturalism as a manifesto of its decolonizing tendencies, the result, to an extent, of the growth of a global economy.[16] This is true of Donald Pease's *National Identities and Post-Americanist Narratives* and, to an extent, of John Carlos Rowe's *The New American Studies*, along with the numerous books and edited collections on this subject mentioned earlier.[17] These anthologies attempt to forge a connection between postcolonialism and the new directions ethnic studies in the US has taken, focusing on border crossing, migration, assimilation and transnationalism, exemplified arguably in the clearest terms in Gloria Anzaldúa's *Borderlands/La Frontera*. Lawrence Buell takes a step backwards and traces 'postcolonial anxiety' in the earliest 'yankee' American texts. Surprisingly, Buell identifies the existence of the tension between standard English and its local deviants in US writing in much the same manner as other critics do in the postcolonial novels of, say, Chinua Achebe or Raja Rao (Buell 2000: 208). Thus he manages to equate Cooper, Emerson, Whitman and Twain with Amos Tutuola, Gabriel Okara and Nissim Ezekiel (Buell 1992: 427, 428).[18] Of course, the Americans adopted primarily British models and 'postcolonially' introduced Americanisms into standard English. It has even been suggested that postcolonial studies in the US is synonymous with W. E. B. Dubois's early text, *The Souls of Black Folk* (see Mostern 2000). Thus, for this motley group of critics, what we now call 'postcolonial critique' was pretty much in existence within American Studies as early as 1903.[19]

In *The New American Studies*, Rowe posits a 'new' American Studies against an 'old' American Studies such that the former does not prey upon the latter, but is more 'comparatist' in nature (Rowe 2002a: xv). The model Rowe proposes is that of Mary Louise Pratt's concept of multicultural 'contact zones' as enumerated in *Profession 91*, which not only includes the study of 'conquest, colonization, revolution, abolition, reconstruction, Manifest Destiny, Indian removal, [and] modernization' but also transcends these traditional aspects to bridge the gap between a customary 'American Studies' and the 'borderlands' of Asia, Canada, Africa and Europe to produce a fitting multiculturalist model (Rowe 2002a: 13, 16, 59). In doing so, Rowe turns 'post-nationalist' American Studies into a generic New American Studies. Such a multidisciplinary project, one would surmise, would sit awkwardly with American exceptionalism since post-ist tendencies that reinforce the postcolonial impulse are meant to check unilateral approaches. Notwithstanding this, a new Americanist canon appears to be on everyone's mind,[20] with the exhortation (as well as the added anxiety) that a cultural studies model may be the way to resist exceptionalist ideologies that offer sweeping US nationalist models as metatheory. But multiculturalist models have risks (that can be turned into advantages) of their own. In the US, ethnicity has become the quintessence of experience and Ethnic Studies the buzz word that is transformed into a definitive 'world literature' with the US at the centre, replacing even comparative literature as a means by which white Americans can contain non-white America. In this context, a sequence of questions can be advanced: Is the US the only country that is multiethnic? Do ethnic societies or ethnic literatures not exist elsewhere? Why is it that we call Indian literature multilingual but never multiethnic or multicultural? Is 'ethnic' a euphemism for the immigrant in the United States? (Trivedi 2010). Not for nothing was the cultural studies curriculum at UCB in the 1980s taken as a sign that the US multicultural society is a 'model for the world' (Rowe 2002a: 74).

Increasingly, however, postcolonial studies in the US has evinced a ground-shift from fixing models of cultural distinctiveness to showing interest in syncretism, ambivalence and globality.[21] In his attempt to explain the sweep of the new American Studies, Rowe appreciates the 'vigilance' and 'possible uses' of this new discipline 'in the cultural imperialist agendas central to US foreign policies from the Marshall Plan in postwar Europe to the multinational alliance *we* assembled to fight (and legitimate) the Gulf War' (Rowe 2002b: 171; my emphasis).[22] The 'writing back' of other cultures as a bulwark against the cultural and economic domination of the US should also be a part of American Studies so that it becomes 'comparatist' (Rowe 2002b: 172). In similar fashion, Rowe writes elsewhere: 'I believe that the futures of both fields are crucially related and that mistaken efforts to struggle with each other for institutional power and space may have unexpectedly negative consequences for both fields' (Rowe 2004: 38). However, he then calls for 'a unified American studies discipline, department, program, and professional organization – which usually means one devoted to some version of nationalist study or American exceptionalism' to avoid getting sidelined by other studies that are concerned with ethnicity, gender, sexuality and the gamut of cultural studies, proposing a method all Americanists should follow: they should not 'rush to defend' American Studies against the teaching/research in minority studies *if* the latter is geared toward serving the Americanist canon' (Rowe 2002b: 173, 174; my emphasis). Here, Rowe pleads for a kind of 'internationalization' of American Studies but with a limited 'regionalism' comprising of local knowledges that permeate mainstream America-supported curricula on the grounds of Buell's even more sentimental but hard-hitting view that although the new American Studies is engaged in 'culture wars' and has to work between models of 'cultural hybridization or syncretism' on the one hand and 'cultural particularism' on the other, to embrace the former would surely amount to 'throwing ourselves wholly, *amor fati*-like, on the pyre of postnationalism (in a kind of subdisciplinary suttee)' (Buell 1996: 89, 91). In other words, although branching out into a new Americanist scholarship by appropriating postcolonialism is a desired goal, it is fraught with concerns about the loss of the American nation and its distinctiveness, meaning also presumably its exceptionalism. The debates of the 1990s, spurred by *The Empire Writes Back*, were commingled, perhaps inadvertently, with the disintegration of the idea of national identity.

Configurations of identity emphasizing an 'us versus them' binary would severely put theories of transnationalism and transculturalism to the test. America's diasporic heterogeneity, and the new global order that fashioned postcolonial theory out of a universe of signs completely disconnected from their social and political provenance, turns out to be affected by xenophobia and national insularity. US multiculturalism and its much-touted diversity shows its restless parochialism when faced with the decanonization of the American genre. In the days following 9/11, in particular, US anxieties led to the reconstruction of barriers, virtual and non-virtual, in a world heretofore declared borderless. Nowadays, it appears that multiculturalism is mere folklore in the face of a discredited authoritarianism of the US nation that is being reproduced increasingly in place of democracy.[23] It is no wonder that Singh and Schmidt describe the US as 'the world's first postcolonial *and* neocolonial country' (Singh and Schmidt 2000: 5).

In spite of the purported cosmopolitanism of Rowe's 'new-Americanist', 'post-nationalist' studies, is America truly postcolonial? That it contains marginalized classes makes it commensurable with any subaltern studies project. But apart from the problematic contrariness of sameness and difference, rampant nationalism and the 'global cultural economy', the United States has also to unscramble the unsettled issues of its own minority discourse of race. In addition, unlike the countries of the decolonized south, the US has to grapple with the impossible task of theorizing about the historical disparity between a prosperous north and an underprivileged south when confronted with the issue of common oppression.[24] Would there be a standoff between the minorities of the third world and the marginalized of the first when they become acculturated? When the United States appropriates the language of postcolonial studies, both the north and the south can, at best, co-exist loosely in a condition of 'postcoloniality'.

Proclamations of hybridity and multiculturalism in the west as parameters of postcolonial studies neglect debates centred around the international division of labour and the role of the political left, which amounts to 'eclecticism' and 'political vagrancy' (Ahmad 1993: 62, 64). Ahmad squarely blames postmodernism for this new expression of postcolonialism. In his view, postcolonial studies became operational in the US once postmodernism had displaced Marxism as an instrument of protest and resistance. Dissent is now articulated through the prism of relativism and fragmentation, which are tropes of textualism, instead of activism and left politics. To have multiculturalism or cultural hybridization serve as the criteria for allowing authors of the American Renaissance an entry into postcolonial studies (as Buell has done) would be a gross injustice to the history of decolonization struggles in the world. The disavowal of logocentrism has led to a disinclination to pursue projects of human liberation, permitting race, class, gender and history to be abandoned in service to 'theory'.

The decline of Marxist struggles, when linked with the rise of corporatism in the academy, throws up the issue of the emergence of postcolonial intellectuals in the west. These postcolonial-postmodern intellectuals, Gikandi's 'émigré native informants' (Gikandi 2001: 646), have opened up shop in the US, shipping a well-packaged 'third-worldism' back to its proponents, further disempowering the politics of identity, individuality and distinctiveness.[25] In Ahmad's view, contemporary theory simply sponsors capitalism by being complicit with it. The nexus might well be an off-shoot of the Thatcherite-Reaganite consensus:

> This consensus, especially aggressive now in the moment of imperialism's greatest triumph in its history, is unwilling to grant any considerable space to fundamental dissent of *any* kind, so that demands even for simple decency – that non-Western texts be integrated into the basic syllabi, that women have the right to abortion or equal pay or the writing of their own history, that normative pressures concede ground to individual sexual

> choice – are construed as mad attacks on Western civilization and 'family values', and as outright degenerations against which 'the American mind', as Alan Bloom tendentiously calls it, needs to defend itself. (Ahmad 1993: 65)

While issues of hybridity and multiculturalism, creolization and cultural diversity, may be well suited to the curricula taught in US universities, once translated into postcolonial studies, they are apt to become disabling for the kinds of struggles waged in the third world, this being one of the primary reasons why postcolonial studies receives so much flak.[26]

Related concerns about the lack of historical precision in using the term 'postcolonial' have ramifications for the state of capitalism that, to a large extent, is responsible for blurring the line between the victor and the vanquished, though one could argue that the line is even more deeply etched today. New configurations of postcolonial studies dispel 'determinate histories of determinate structures' such that we are offered 'a globalized *condition* of postcoloniality' in which 'determinate forms of struggle' are sacrificed in favour of 'domains of discourse and pedagogy' (Ahmad 1995b: 31). Within such terms, the status of the United States as postcolonial is severely challenged. To address the history of the US in the manner of the histories of the decolonized nations since the Second World War 'strains the definition of the postcolonial, which implies a temporal development (from "colonial" to "post") that relies heavily on the spatial coordinates of European empires, in their formal acquisition of territories and the subsequent history of decolonization and national independence' (Kaplan 1993: 17).

Thus, to be effective, postcolonial studies must acquire a different *avatar* in the US, linked to its transnational capitalism and the corporatization of every aspect of culture so that postcolonialism and transnationalism become easily distinguishable. Postcolonialism, as a 'period term' (Boehmer 1995: 3), when used with a hyphen to indicate 'after colonialism', stands for freedom from colonization and inspires confidence in the identity of the nation. But when used without a hyphen, it is indicative of a continuation of colonialism which is best exemplified by the

United States. Thus put, the third-world nation-state appears to be the prize victim that is sacrificed at the altar of a neocolonialism masquerading as postcolonialism.

The question to be posed, then, is whether Buell's 'postcolonial anxiety' has finally worked itself out and come to a conclusion. One cannot deny that owing to the absence of any political standpoint, postcolonial theory has effectually become borderless theory. Although there are racial and ethnic matters to be considered in the United States, the risk of a homogeneous, over-arching, already stretched, label of postcolonial studies spanning a rampant cultural imperialism would be a doomed project. There tends to be an uneasy engagement between political and academic positions which, in terms of my own study, could well mean the end of national sensibility and a subservience to Americanism through global exchange.

5

CONCLUSION: NEW DIRECTIONS

Postcolonial studies has been, by and large, consistent with the fashion of dismissing what one may call 'the politics of engagement' in third-world nation-states. When postcolonialism emerged, it was geared to understanding the insidious ways of the new imperialism as much as to the interpretation of colonial histories, which had been its conservative function. However, postcolonial studies has flourished since the 'defeat or perversion of national liberation movements in exploited countries all over the world' and the decline of radical politics in decolonized nation-states (Hallward 2001: xiv). Ever since the United States overcame its Cold War hostilities, with capitalism trouncing Marxism, postcolonial studies has established affinities with the third-world expatriate, forsaking its larger liberatory concerns. Furthermore, it has become important to determine the value of postcolonialism as a counter to the processes of globalization.

In response to the question, 'how might a valid postcolonial practice be advanced?', it should first be noted that the location of theories of decolonization and the task of rewriting histories within the academy have been conducted through the well-rehearsed medium of literature, which is a significant channel for the study of social and political struggles. Though I have focused here on postcolonial studies as part of university curricula, particularly when addressing its emergence in the United States, what is even more important are the extra-literary concerns that can help link postcolonialism with activism in the world outside the academy. That is why I have chosen to view postcolonialism not only as an academic discipline constituted of theories taught in the university but also as a practice based on a critique of globalization that might arrest the shrinking significance of the nation-state. In other words, a revolutionary struggle or a mammoth rally against the Iraq war will be considered as postcolonial moments because postcolonialism is grounded in this register of activism. That is why it has been important to distinguish between postcolonialism, postcolonial theory and postcolonial studies, the last two being reviled most severely by Marxist critics. Indeed, if postcolonial studies were to represent the history of exploitation, struggle and resistance, there would be no need to make such distinctions.

The dozens of books on postcolonialism that appeared in the late 1980s and throughout the 1990s traced the origins of post-colonialism from decolonization struggles to the current climate of rampant globalization perpetrated primarily by the United States. Many of these genealogical texts found links between the various 'posts' dominating theory today, which allowed critics like Ahmad, Dirlik and San Juan, Jr. – to name just three – to uncover a complicity between western theory and representations of third-world struggles. The two-way street between western hegemony and postcolonial studies is underscored by concepts such as 'cultural hybridity' and 'multiculturalism' which have Americanized postcolonial studies, adding chaos to confusion. Admittedly, it is all too easy to indulge in mudslinging against the United States as the progenitor of the economic dimension of globalization, but academically too, it has been condemned for patronizing third-world intellectuals and for turning ethnic studies into a form of postcolonial studies that, in turn, does not represent third-world struggles. Multiculturalism dissolves the impermeability of first and third worlds and acts as a cover for US crimes that continue to be perpetrated in tune with the ancient binaries regardless of any academic advances in the university.

In its new American guise, postcolonial studies is also accused of spatial dislocation, while in its third-world configuration, the 'postcolonial' has lost its validity as the visible structures of nationhood are systematically dismantled by theories of postcolonialism. The turn in postcolonialism renders redundant one of the most significant categories of identity politics – the nation. The success of information technology and the internet, the global spread of transnational corporations and the flows of capital, make us wonder where labour is currently located. Whereas labour and trade unions had been the primary focus of Marxist struggles, they are now lost in the maze of global exchange. The triumph of globalization over labour and the nation, categories that were quintessential to decolonizing struggles, has led the opponents of postcolonial studies to object that there appears to be no historical or materialist trajectory in such writing, just as there is an enormous rift between its anticolonial 'intellectual antecedents' such as C. L. R. James, Fanon, Césaire, Gandhi, Nyrere, Senghor, Memmi, Cabral and others and the more contemporary breed of intellectuals known as postcolonial theorists (Sharpe 2000a: 109).

The hegemony of American curricula across the universities of the world, the migration of postcolonial theorists to the United States, the role of the US as 'leader of the free world', and the shift from the national to the global have resulted in postcolonialism – as we knew it – being virtually left in the cold. The dismantling of binarisms has proved to be a mixed blessing. Postcolonial studies, guided as it is by a postmodernist agenda, has already entered the debate on end-ism. With the 'end of history', there can scarcely be any future for resistance movements in the postcolonial world. To have been unhooked from its moorings in history, and thereby from the oppressive systems in world hierarchy, has proven to be the greatest setback to studies in postcolonialism. One has to agree with Benita Parry that

> the time has come for postcolonial studies to promote empirical investigations of these unsettled diasporas, and undertake the dissemination of the experiences spoken by scattered, impoverished, and despised populations stranded in temporary and exploited employment as contract workers, casual laborers, or domestic servants in Europe, North America, and the Gulf States. (Parry 2002: 72)

These 'empirical investigations' are necessary to recover voices of dissent and resistance that can be well nigh lost in the sweeping wave of 'corporatization'. At least ideologically, if not practically, the persuasions of globalization and the role of the World Trade Organization, the International Monetary Fund and the

World Bank must be adequately theorized and singularly held responsible for ecological degradation, the spread of HIV and food insecurities, the lack of funding for more widespread literacy, and the contamination of water, among other disasters in the third world. As a rule, globalization is the term used to cover trade and economic transactions and agreements between governments. As it has been used in this book, however, the term designates the processes that have caused rifts between those who have the talent to prosper in global markets and those who perceive it as deeply inimical to firmly held principles and ideologies.[1]

We are facing a peculiar impasse today: in order to ensure the success of protest and political action, the enemy has to be identified. While this might still be possible in the real world, the enemy has been obscured in high academia. Academic postcolonialism has obfuscated globalization with the misty discourse of a lexicon which seems to promise freedom. The consciousness of being part of a nation was undeniably a result of freedom from the Enlightenment binaries of core and periphery, facilitated by postcolonial thought, until the nation itself became the enemy. As freedoms began to be interrogated, national structures in newly independent countries themselves became suspect. Postcolonialism was the new guru which shook complacencies until another enemy was identified – globalization – which, however, went hand in hand with what had, by then, begun to be called Colonial Discourse Analysis. As it became evident that in a fully transnational world there was no longer any 'nation', no cultural specificity, no identity even, postcolonial theorists began a celebration of sorts. Binarism, when filtered through postcolonial theory, was duly discovered to be profoundly untenable.

But when categories of colonizer/colonized dissolve, so do structures of oppression and domination. In such an environment, movements of counter-globalization raise issues of victims and victimizers only to be silenced by the blithe discourse of globalization. Upbeat as ever, Hardt and Negri write: 'Today ... we can see that the traditional forms of resistance, such as the institutional workers' organizations that developed through the major part of the nineteenth and twentieth centuries have begun to lose their power' (Hardt and Negri 2000: 308).[2] Despite exhortations of resistance and their attempts to maintain links with Marx, the celebratory note where global capital is concerned is hard to miss: 'The traditional idea of counter-power and the idea of resistance against modern sovereignty in general thus becomes less and less possible' (Hardt and Negri 2000: 308). For Hardt, the global oppositionists constitute a 'sea of people' that are 'unknowable, chaotic, dispersive' (Hardt 2002: 113); their struggles can have no focused target: 'We maintain ... that today this localist position, although we admire and respect the spirit of some of its proponents, is both false and damaging' (Hardt and Negri 2000: 44). In a short essay on the World Social Forum at Porto Alegre, Hardt presents two alternatives for opponents of globalization: either the 'sovereignty of nation-states' or the 'non-national alternative' of 'democratic globalization' can be employed against global capital (Hardt 2002: 114). The former is outmoded and outdated and no amount of nostalgia for the faded power structures of the nation-state need be evoked (Hardt 2002: 114; Hardt and Negri 2000: 43–4). The latter includes struggle but within the domain of postcapitalism. The prime difficulty is to 'determine the enemy against which to rebel' and discover the 'production of oppression' (Hardt and Negri 2000: 210–11) since rebellion is not aimed at the capitalist class, employers or the state. The issue the authors raise frequently is whether there is an enemy at all. In the context of a global revolution initiated by the 'multitude' that is fashioned out of the 'people', there would be little relevance of local struggles, provincial nationalisms or alternative world models. If one is an advocate of swimming with the tide, how can others be inspired to go against it? The message is implicit: capital is such a monolithic force that opposition to it is futile. Hardt and Negri's endorsement of the role of the WTO and the IMF in safeguarding and regulating capital flows and their overall sanguineness in the face of globalization prompts the question whether small, local struggles at the point of production can be at all successful in countering the massive flows of global capital working their way through transnational corporations.

To that question, however, many instances of resistance that have advocated the imagining of an alternative world can be cited, among them the Zapatista protestors' unique and subversive postcolonial gesture of releasing hundreds of paper aeroplanes at the 2001 G8 summit in Genoa. Symbolically, these paper planes fashioned by school children, bearing messages from the Zapatista neighbourhood, became a way of bypassing and transgressing the fences erected by the leaders of the western world. The Zapatista movement – which is not a national movement nor does it promote any grand design – is engaged in a war against free-trade negotiations which has begun to inspire other protestors around the world. The 1999 rallies that interrupted the WTO summit in Seattle – convened to frame policies on privatization, patenting and intellectual property rights – is another exemplary case.[3] Similarly, there are myriad demonstrations and movements going on in different pockets of the world: in Nigeria, for instance, the Ogoni people are fighting to recover their land from Shell Oil; in India, the supporters of the Narmada Bachao Andolan and those who are affected by it constantly agitate against the regular doses of funding the project receives from the World Bank. The rallies and strikes in many parts of the world against agri-businesses like monocultural farming, patenting and biopiracy, campaigns to prevent deforestation and the construction of Special Economic Zones as in Bengal in India, the protests against massive privatization of resources and those against the US-controlled structural adjustment programmes, along with so much more, are all part of the worldwide movement against globalization. Thus, so-called anti-globalization movements can be appreciated for creating a consciousness among people about the impact of rapacious capitalism. Rather than simply accepting it as the way of the world, conscientious citizens can debate about alternatives to it. Without this, only the left, the intellectuals, the worker's movements and the environmentalists would appear to be the ones mindful of globalization's subterranean dimensions.

In all these cases, the obvious adversary is the state, although Hardt and Negri appear to be confused on this issue. But there are occasions when the state takes up the cause of its citizens, despite Hardt and Negri's denunciation of national solidarity: the measures taken by the Malaysian government to check excessive capital investment in 1997–98 rather than go the way of Indonesia, South Korea and Thailand, and the refusal to accept hybrid seeds from Monsanto by several African governments (Mertes 2003: 152) are examples of state-supported agitation. The arrangement of the massive World Social Forum meetings in Porto Alegre in 2002 – where 51,300 people from 131 countries, including 4,909 organizations were brought together – and elsewhere is itself a sign of the strength of the state that assists in institutionalizing censure against itself. It would be quite meaningless to engage in such political struggles if the nation-state were dead.

Hardt and Negri's book is allegedly about hope and optimism for the rise of resistance in the world, though the creation of new subjectivities is nowhere clear. Their wistfulness for resistance may be attractive to both Marxists and postcolonialists, but what sort of a resistance do they have in mind? Bartolovich poses a range of polemical issues (published prior to *Empire*) that are relevant to the nature of resistance as discussed by the two authors:

> Does an *articulation* of struggles (antiracist, antipatriarchal, proletarian...) require a different 'form' than the 'proletarian struggle'? What about diaspora? When 'national' populations are dispersed, what 'form' does struggle take? Can there be 'transnational' sites of resistance? What would they look like? What 'form' furthers most effectively 'globalization from below' – the formation of transnational alliances among unions and other groups resisting corporate globalization? (Bartolovich 2000: 148).

One could add to the list some basic human concerns such as health care, the alleviation of poverty and the spread of literacy, all of which are linked to the significance of the political soundness of the state. For the authors of *Empire*, however, opposition is of the formless type. Their appeals to a 'new type of resistance' that 'would be adequate to the new dimensions of sovereignty' (Hardt and Negri 2000: 308) remain mysterious. Likewise, their strategies of counter-power are obscure and many of their discussions of protest struggles are ambiguous. The book also contains bleak messages such as the following:

> Even when we manage to touch on the productive, ontological dimension of the problematic and the resistances that arise there, however, we will still not be in the position – *not even at the end of this book* – to point to any already existing and concrete elaboration of a political alternative to Empire. And no such effective blueprint will ever arise from a theoretical articulation such as ours. (Hardt and Negri 2000: 206; my emphasis)

Thus the authors openly admit that those readers who reach the end of the book will not find an 'effective blueprint' that will serve as a guide to an effectual and comprehensive resistance.[4] This cannot but imply the inexorable nature of processes of globalization in relation to which the nation-state will be merely a facilitator and unable to stand in the way.

Within this gloomy picture, Hardt and Negri's interpretation of the 'multitude' that will 'magically rise up to inherit the earth' (Harvey 2003: 169) also bespeaks of homogeneity and indifference to variations in strategies of protest. It runs the risk of edging out local, irregular models of resistance owing to its affinity with some kind of uniform and horizontal 'network', a kind of organization of diverse groups that are non-contradictory and very much in tune with the 'non-national alternative' of 'democratic globalization' (Hardt 2002: 114). Again, as an extremely diffuse idea offering no solution for the moment, it does seem to relate to Appadurai's description of technoscapes – the exchange of global economics on a super-fast scale without any semblance of political control or hierarchy (Appadurai 2000: 1807). Bhabha's succession of images of the self that problematize identity as well as Friedman's 'electronic herd' where 'no one is in charge' belong in the same league (Bhabha 1994: 77; Friedman 2000: 112–13). The 'multitude', for Hardt and Negri, has always asserted itself in this manner.

In many respects, such a dystopic view of nation-states makes oppositional struggles even more important as the most effective way of bridging 'the gap between economic circuits and political sovereignty' (Meiksins Wood 2003: 81).[5] Nowhere is the justification for rebellion and revolution reaffirmed more powerfully than in the utter failure of globalization in Latin

America, which completely ruined the economies of Brazil, Argentina, Venezuela and Uruguay.[6] On the other hand, the struggles that led to the setting up of the Kyoto treaty, instituted to ward off the effects of global warming, at least gesture towards the beginning of a dialogue between the global masters and activists and put the defenders of globalization on the defensive. It is heartening to know that the state of Seattle cut back massively on its carbon emissions over the last decade, despite the Bush administration's announcement in 2003 that it planned to tackle the growing energy crisis by increasing coal mining and oil production as alternative sources of energy.[7] The occasional victory of a lone Green Party candidate in parts of the western world also indicates that there are supporters everywhere (Aronowitz 2003: 195). Sooner or later, the 'global' world will have to come to terms with environmental destruction and impose severe limits on the pollution linked with industrial growth. Oxfam's injunction to 'make poverty history' – involving a worldwide coalition of agencies that focus on aid and development – or Nelson Mandela's appeal in Trafalgar Square to the leaders of the G8 countries to acknowledge that the 'world is hungry for action, not words', were not uttered without an awareness of victims and victimizers.

But September 2001 was a turning point for champions of globalization as it gave them the opportunity to link terrorism with activism. This act of violence strengthened American patriotism to the hilt and gave legitimacy to the ensuing 'war on terror'. Global thinking post-9/11 changed so radically that war seemed to become the only means of maintaining order. Bush's theory of a new 'Axis of Evil' consisting of Middle Eastern and Asian countries had an impact on many concepts relating to struggle and activism:

> In the service of the new militarism, all other concerns, including poverty and constitutional protections such as civil liberties and civil rights – indeed, the right to dissent from official policy – [became] not only subordinate to the advancing war machine but ... suspect on patriotic grounds. And the labor movement ... experience[d] new threats to its independence, especially the right to strike as the American president

threaten[ed] to abrogate its exercise on national security grounds. (Aronowitz and Gautney 2003: xxx)

During the Bush regime, US-sponsored globalization practically became synonymous with the 'war on terror' and the militarized repression of its antagonists. But even in the post-Bush world, economic globalization has metamorphosed into a full-scale global war in which Israel, China, Russia and the once non-aligned India speak in unison to support the United States. The pressures of US unilateralism everywhere have led to the invasions of Iraq and Afghanistan, resulting in the deaths of thousands, including children.[8] The Israeli atrocities in Palestine, with encouragement from the US, are also linked to post-9/11 terrorism. In other words, the war against terror has proved to be a formidable weapon in spurring nations to come harking back to the US, losing their capacity for independent judgement in the process.[9]

Even among intellectuals, only a few people, such as Edward Said, probed America's unprecedented aggression: 'This is a war against terrorism, everyone says, but where, on what fronts, for what concrete ends? No answers are provided, except the vague suggestion that the Middle East and Islam are what "we" are up against, and that terrorism must be destroyed' (Said 2001). Chomsky's criticism of the role of the US is also well articulated: 'The National Security Strategy declared that the United States – alone – has the right to carry out "preventive war": preventive, not preemptive, using military force to eliminate a perceived threat, even if invented or imagined' (Chomsky 2007: 36). Regarding the effects of 9/11 on globalization, Chomsky writes: 'Such terrorist atrocities are a gift to the harshest and most repressive elements on all sides, and are sure to be exploited – already have been in fact – to accelerate the agenda of militarization, regimentation, reversal of social democratic programs, transfer of wealth to narrow sectors, and undermining democracy in any meaningful form' (Chomsky 2001: 19).

Sure enough, the dead of the twin towers of the World Trade Center were used shamelessly by Robert Zoellick, currently president of the World Bank, who was at the time trade representative of the US, when he declared:

> On 11 September, America, its open society, and its ideas came under attack by a malevolence that craves our panic, retreat, and abdication of global leadership ... This President and this administration will fight for open markets. We will not be intimidated by those who have taken to the streets to blame trade – and America – for the world's ills. (Cited in Notes 2003: 501).

In one stroke, Zoellick was given carte blanche to make terrorists out of activists and to proclaim the end of anti-globalization resistance. A country so traumatized that it would accept government policy unhesitatingly and help usher in 'a free market paradise' may well have been the major side-effect of 9/11 (Žižek 2009: 18). The appropriation of 'the language of national self-protection' twists the issue of promoting neoliberalism into a 'defence of America's "human rights" universalism', thereby changing the complexion of anti-imperialist struggles (Jameson 2000: 66). Further, the spiralling of the particular into the universal lends support to American exceptionalism as the US becomes aggrandized, and begins to approximate to the global system. The expression of resentment towards those convening the World Economic Forum summit in New York City a few months after 9/11 by the simultaneous holding of the World Social Forum summit in Porto Alegre, where enormous rallies were organized to protest globalization, becomes all the more significant. It reiterates active commitment to a cause.

The years following 2001 saw millions of demonstrators join together to condemn the invasion of Iraq by the United States and its allies. As the *New York Times* noted: 'The huge antiwar demonstrators around the world this weekend are reminders that there may still be two superpowers on the planet: the United States and world public opinion' (Tyler 2003). In terms of the anachronistic binaries of postcolonialism, we might say that anti-globalization movements are, in fact, the peripheries working to displace the centre. The great majority of people who constitute the periphery come from formerly colonized countries. As far as the common people in those countries are concerned, the enthusiasm for a better life free of corporate control still exists.

It is their governments who fall prey to the controlling interests of the west.

The turning point in Hardt and Negri's *Empire* is the warning against the inevitable failures of resistance per se. Resistance becomes mere recklessness unless it is turned into a collective enterprise, as in national integration movements or the extraordinary student protests of the 1960s, especially the Free Speech Movement at the University of California, Berkeley, and the student agitation at the Sorbonne in Paris. Mass demonstrations cannot continue on their own unless issues relating to class, race, gender, ecological protection and even diasporic patterns are thoroughly politicized. When Hardt and Negri speak about the exemplary struggles of the Zapatistas as a form of resistance to Empire, they too must address related issues such as environmentalism and feminism that intersect and create an unevenness in the politics of protest.[10] No doubt, proletarian-led struggles have been remarkably successful within the nation-state, but owing to the disengagement of working-class movements from other dynamic struggles, the Marxist concept of the proletariat has lost much of its power – as witnessed in South-East Asia, particularly Indonesia, where socialist movements were severely repressed in 1965 as Suharto deposed Sukarno amidst a saturnalia of blood (Harvey 2003: 171). After 1973 particularly, working-class movements became more-or-less inadequate to the task of frustrating capital accumulation and rapid privatization. But the alternative struggles that replaced them were also indeterminate and confused, and were often in conflict with the socialist-based traditional left. Though they form part of the anti-globalization movement and are against neoliberalism in temper, the trade-unionist policies of the left often conflict with the local and loose nature of alternative struggles.

The only way to ensure that resistance remains possible lies in urgently reviving the nation-state. Alongside that, in the present context, it will involve the intellectual exercise of transforming postcolonial studies so that it becomes capable of incorporating resistance against postmodernism's unsettling tendencies. Undoubtedly, the nation-state is a very problematic category and nationalism a lop-sided homogeneous discourse propped up by a popular bourgeois ideology (see Sethi 1999), yet it might be the only political formation able to mitigate the unprecedented poverty and discrimination, violence and civil strife, that are the results of globalization and of the geo-political interventions of the west. The state is the only possible means of maintaining public confidence in the securities of a healthy and clean environment with easy access to sources of energy and water, employment, education and a decent standard of living. But the state would have to be 'a fully empowered representative interstate organization', something the United Nations could have been were it not for its subordination to the US, in order to keep a watchful eye on the self-serving industrial nations of the north and to remove friction when their interests collide with those of the south (Miyoshi 1997: 55–6). The state would also have to support the grassroots activities of non-governmental organizations so that they can withstand the sweeping powers of the TNCs. Finally, the need for labour unions at the transnational level would have to be met by the state. Only networks of alliances among the workers of the world could militate against the invincibility of corporatism (Miyoshi 1997: 56).

This book has retreated from current theories of discourse and raised questions relating to oppression and resistance in an attempt to give a historical-materialist twist to postcolonial studies. Rather than wildly condemning postcolonial approaches to society, culture and literature, or try to bury them prematurely, I have tried to show how nation, globalization, and the new postcolonialism of the United States cannot be dealt with in isolation from the history of third-world struggles. An affiliation between third-world cultures and their social and political histories has to be established so that postcolonial studies might profitably survive. If certain key aspects of postcolonial studies – nationalism, globalization, the subaltern – are issues that Marxists have been involved in from the beginning, why should postcolonialist practitioners be reluctant to embrace Marxist parameters?

Highlighting the significance of resistance and activism in the third world as being primarily Marxist concerns does not, however, diminish the contribution of postcolonial studies to revisionism, especially with regard to the colonial past. Despite their disinheritance of the nation, culturalist interpretations of national formations offer compelling arguments that frustrate the thesis of stable, collective identities relating to class, gender, race and subalternity.[11] As was acknowledged earlier, through its critique of essentialism postcolonial studies demystifies all kinds of structures of domination and grand narratives, especially eurocentrism, to make colonialism a metaphor for all systems of oppression. No one can deny that concerns about globalization were present in one of its earliest texts, *Orientalism*.[12] Again, Spivak can be cited as an example of one of those rare postcolonial theorists who try to balance metropolitan living with the politics of location by falling incessantly into the 'confessional mode' when addressing the question of subalternity.[13] In one of her essays, she refers to the benevolence of the first-world intellectual in writing about the third-world native (Spivak 1988a: 253), just as elsewhere she attempts to highlight the disempowerment of women within the international division of labour underscoring the debilitating effects of globalization (Spivak 1993). To give Spivak her due, it has to be said that despite her emphasis on textuality she has unequivocally opposed the political economy of imperialism.

At this point, postcolonial studies would do well to pause for a moment before settling into its place in the metropolitan curriculum. With regard to oppression and resistance, points of intersection might be discovered between postcolonialism and Marxism at precisely such moments. With their guard lowered and hostilities downscaled, both methodologies should acknowledge each other 'in mutual sites of concern, and concede to the field the authentic insights and advances that have been generated within it' (Bartolovich 2002: 10). Fortunately, Bartolovich uses 'authentic' without scare quotes. It is not as though imbalances will vanish if and when Marxism becomes synchronized with postcolonialism, but we shall at least cease to think that prosperity is global or that globalization has indeed vastly reduced the divide between the first and the third worlds.

NOTES

Chapter One

1. In the 1995 'Afterword' to *Orientalism*, Said distinguishes postcolonialism as-it-used-to-be from postcolonialism as-it-has-evolved, having moved from the writings of 'distinguished thinkers as Anwar Abdel Malek, Samir Amin, C. L. R. James' to those of its more postmodernist practitioners, and from themes of struggle and liberation to a detachment from urgent political goals: 'The earliest studies of the post-colonial ... were based on studies of domination and control made from the standpoint of either a completed political independence or an incomplete liberationist project. Yet whereas post-modernism in one of its most famous programmatic statements (by Jean-François Lyotard) stresses the disappearance of the grand narratives of emancipation and enlightenment, the emphasis behind much of the work done by the first generation of post-colonial artists and scholars is exactly the opposite: the grand narratives remain, even though their implementation and realization are at present in abeyance, deferred, or circumvented. This crucial difference between the urgent historical and political imperatives of post-colonialism and post-modernism's relative detachment makes for altogether different approaches and results' (Said 1995: 351).
2. To misquote what McQuillan et al. have said: 'Nothing stimulates the production of postcolonialism like the proclamation of its own death, regardless of who makes the proclamation' (McQuillan et al. 1999: ix).
3. For John McLeod, postcolonial theory has 'conceded too much ground by questioning oppositional discourses such as nationalism and Marxism *at the very moment* when we need these discourses more than ever to combat conflicts around the world' (McLeod 2000: 252). The inverse is as true. As Young puts it: 'in practice postcolonial studies can be strongly foundationalist, grounded in an epistemology which gives primacy to an authentic historical reality (a position decisively mapped out in the founding text of modern postcolonial studies, Edward Said's *Orientalism* of 1978)' (Young 1998: 7–8).

4. As Ahmad writes: '[Only] those critics, who believe not only that colonialism has more or less ended but who also subscribe to the idea of the end of Marxism, nationalism, collective historical subjects and revolutionary possibility as such, are the *true* post-colonials, while the rest of us, who do not quite accept this apocalyptic anti-Marxism, are not postcolonial at all' (Ahmad 1995a: 10).
5. Darshan Perusekh goes so far as to consider postcolonial studies a 'finished' product built on 'raw material' taken from the former colonies and later 'shipped back' to it for utilization (cited in M. Mukherjee 1996: 10).
6. Dirlik claims that in this respect it is deceptive 'to classify as postcolonial critics intellectuals as widely different politically as Edward Said, Aijaz Ahmad, Homi Bhabha, Gyan Prakash, Gayatri Spivak, and Lata Mani. In a literal sense, they may all share in post-coloniality and some of its themes. Said's situation as a Palestinian intellectual does not permit him to cross the borders of Israel with the ease that his in-betweenness might suggest (which also raises the question for postcolonial critics of what borders are at issue). Ahmad, vehemently critical of the Three Worlds concept, nevertheless grounds his critique within the operations of capital, which is quite different from Prakash's denial of a foundational status to capitalism. Spivak and Mani, though quite cognizant of the different roles in different contexts that in-betweenness imposes upon them, nevertheless ground their politics firmly in feminism (and, in the case of Spivak, Marxism)' (Dirlik 1994: 338–9).
7. Many would say, however, that third-world critics and writers who have made the west their home remain steadfast in their mission despite drawing an American salary. Salman Rushdie has been criticized for seeking British, and now American, protection from the 'barbaric' forces of Islamic fatwas, but the superpowers have not been able to silence his voice when he stridently questions American forays into Afghanistan and Iraq or their double-standards in urging India or Iran to ensure nuclear non-proliferation. On the other hand, allowing marginal dissent and dissidence may be taken as a new form of American liberalism.
8. As Neil Lazarus comments on Bhabha's interpretation of Fanon: 'Bhabha's Fanon would have been unrecognisable to Fanon himself' (Lazarus 1997: 42)
9. In terms of notions of identity, Spivak's anxiety about the appropriation of the subaltern by elite approaches aiming at the recovery of the subaltern's site of desire brings her up against not simply the voicelessness of the gendered subaltern but also the claim that the voice of the representer is always laden with 'benevolence'

when he/she becomes nostalgic for lost origins (Spivak 1988b: 289, 291).

10. As Parry writes: 'Spivak in her own writings severely restricts (eliminates?) the space in which the colonized can be written back into history, even when "interventionist possibilities" are exploited through the deconstructive strategies devised by the post-colonial intellectual' (Parry 1987: 39).
11. Postcolonialism has lost its specificity to such an extent that even London, the capital of the empire upon which the sun never set, is now called a postcolonial city (Ahmad 1995b: 31).
12. Eagleton defines two kinds of postcolonialisms: one that recognizes that most parts of the world had been colonized and that domination still continues in economic, if not political, ways; and the other which is affiliated to western critical theory from where it takes its origin. He writes: 'For myself, it is not that there is no post-colonialism, rather that there is something called postcolonialism and ... something called "postcolonialism" too. That is to say, there is obviously a lot of the globe which used to be colonized directly and is now colonized by other means, a distinction which involves (though it doesn't reduce itself to) one between the political and the economic. At the same time, there is a particular theoretical agenda known as "postcolonialism", which has its roots in a highly specific western intellectual history and is a much more controversial phenomenon altogether. The first kind of postcolonialism has the advantage of being fairly self-evident, along with the drawback of being blandly unarguable; the second kind reaps the benefit of contentiousness, along with the disadvantage of being more easily questioned' (Eagleton 1998: 25).
13. In 'Can the Subaltern Speak?', the essay being referred to, Spivak rejects the subaltern voice on the pretext that one cannot tell whether the nativist demands for nationality, ethnic self-consciousness, mythology, or cultural distinctiveness, as yet unrelated to modes of self-conceptualization within her own culture, are not imbricated with western categories of nationalism or even shades of imperialism. To fall back upon 'third worldism' or native purism is to not get out of the double-bind threatening representationality (Spivak 1988b). As Spivak says in an interview, a 'conscientious ethnography' that celebrates nativism has also to consider that 'the pure native is *not* some necessarily benevolent and good para-human creature, who is there to give us evidence that we must always trust' (Koundoura 1989: 93). To embrace 'third-worldist' notions of the self or bring back the 'native informant syndrome' is to engage in a new sort of orientalism or neocolonialism in the endeavour to generate political

potency (Koundoura 1989: 84). It can be contested, however, that postcolonialism itself may be interpreted as participating in a neo-colonialist hegemony in which the third world is disquietingly theorized into silence. The assertion that the retrieval of native voices or third-worldism is tainted may be a case of the interpreter silencing the subaltern, deferring in his or her own writing an investigation of the history of native agency. By citing the powerful example of *sati*, Spivak, for instance, risks overlooking the presence of other realities. Not only does she limit the hearing of enunciative voices with her sweeping use of poststructuralism, she paradoxically builds up woman as *sati* to the exclusion of her other roles and articulations. Contrary to Spivak, the history of such struggles, especially in their specificity, cannot be shrugged off as a nostalgia for lost origins.

14. Women in India at that time were married off usually before the age of nine or ten. After much debate, the nineteenth-century Brahmin pundits allowed the Age of Consent bill to raise the age of a girl's marriage to 12.
15. Hall's writing on the translation of cultures is well-known in this regard: 'in terms of any absolute return to a pure set of uncontaminated origins, the long-term historical and cultural effects of the "transculturation" which characterised the colonising experience proved ... to be irreversible. The differences, of course, between colonising and colonised cultures remain profound. But they have never operated in a purely binary way and they certainly do so no longer' (Hall 1996: 246–7). Bhabha's emphasis on the unnamed and undefined spaces between opposite taxonomies also questions and restricts the unproblematized power/knowledge relationship that establishes colonial control and mastery. Bhabha's *The Location of Culture* consists of several essays examining how history is always enacted 'between-the-lines', and how colonial discourse can never be unambiguously one-sided – it remains open-ended, comprising of both fear and attraction, sameness and difference (see 'Sly Civility' in Bhabha 1994: 95–6; and especially 'Of Mimicry and Man: The Ambivalence of Colonial Discourse' in Bhabha 1994: 85–92). The traces and left-overs of identity are enacted in a 'third space', an imprecise location where both the postponement of meaning and its restoration can take place (for an understanding of the term 'third space', see Bhabha 1990a: 211). Even Abu-Lughod, who is otherwise a proponent of world-system theory, argues that 'multiple cores are proliferating and some cultural power differences are actually decreasing' (Abu-Lughod 1991: 131).
16. 'There is a "politics" there', Hall writes, 'but it is not one from which complexity and ambiguity can be usefully expunged' (Hall 1996:

244). Hall's argument ties up with the thesis of moral uncertainty presented by Baudrillard in *The Gulf War Did Not Take Place* (1995), where he argues that the war itself was a reconstruction, as in a video game, where it was impossible to distinguish fact from fiction and the real from the hyperreal.

17. See, for instance, Shohat (1992), McClintock (1993), Dirlik (1994), Slemon (1994) and Arun P. Mukherjee (1996).
18. Even Dirlik, towards the end of 'The Postcolonial Aura', acknowledges that 'postcoloniality represents a response to a genuine need, the need to overcome a crisis of understanding produced by the inability of old categories to account for the world' (Dirlik 1994: 352).
19. In responding to globalization, Marxism questioned the role of postcolonial critiques that have 'abandoned "materialist" imperatives for "culturalist" ones [to the extent that they] can no longer properly analyse exploitation and domination – indeed sometimes [do] not even seem to be able to *see* it' (Bartolovich 2000: 146). As Terry Eagleton writes, mockingly: '"Postcolonialism", like postmodernism in general, is among other things a brand of culturalism, which inflates the significance of cultural factors in human affairs. ... It finds it hard to accept that the acknowledgement of difference, hybridity, multiplicity, is a drastically impoverished kind of political ethic, even if the former is of course a *sine qua non* of the latter' (Eagleton 1998: 26).
20. In a chapter entitled 'Derrida in Algeria', Young advances arguments which effectively separate postcolonial practice from postcolonial studies or theory, although he does not make such distinctions. Countering Ahmad, he writes: 'Those who reject contemporary postcolonial theory in the name of the "Third World" on the grounds of it being western however, are themselves in doing so negating the very input of the Third World, starting with Derrida, disavowing therefore the very non-European work which their critique professes to advocate' (Young 2001: 413). By emphasizing the 'non-European' contribution of Derrida's writing, Young does unwittingly accept that the more contemporary 'global' manifestation of postcolonialism is eurocentric and disengaged from praxis.
21. I take Young to be writing from a pro-Marxist stance when he traces postcolonialism's genesis to Algeria. But for Parry, Young appears to be 'placing deconstruction amongst "the great tricontinental anti-colonial intellectual" traditions according to which the Marxist legacy was transformed within postcolonial studies', or worse still, 'displacing Marxism with deconstruction' (Parry 2004b: 7).
22. Young argues that both structuralism and poststructuralism were 'fundamentally anti-western in strategy' to start with, and were only

later identified with Europe. He writes: 'Postcolonial thought has combined the radical heritage of such theory with further ideas and perspectives from tricontinental writers, together with other writers who have emigrated from decolonised tricontinental countries to the west' (Young 2001: 68). Young has objections to the use of the phrase 'third world' because it is a rolling stone gathering adjectives like illiteracy, backwardness, civil strife and, of course, destitution and deprivation. He uses an alternative – 'tricontinental' – a term denoting the three continents of the south. Used first by Anouar Abdel-Malek in 1966 at the Organization of Solidarity of the Peoples of Africa, Asia and Latin America at Havana, 'tricontinental' avoids the pitfalls of the term 'postcolonial' (Young 2001: 4–5). Although Young substitutes 'tricontinental' for 'third world', he nowhere advocates US-sponsored postcolonialism as the norm.

23. Reversing Said's well-rehearsed thesis that orientalist stereotypes and imperial motives are complicit, Young defends western academic institutions for possessing the open-mindedness to encourage studies that seek to undermine the west itself (Young 2001: 63).
24. In the light of the increasing politicization of the discipline and the spur it has provided to its multifarious related fields, Ahmad's criticism of the 'location politics' of postcolonial critics itself carries the risk of homogenization. Who among the intellectuals living in the west, especially those coming from the third world, can be excluded from his gaze? Partha Chatterjee believes that Ahmad himself is no saint since he is as culpable of residing in the west as any of the native intellectuals he criticizes. Chatterjee has written: 'I am struck by the fact that for someone so concerned with institutional site and individual location, Aijaz's book should conceal so strenuously, in its jacket, preliminary pages and text, the fact that the author has spend the overwhelming part of his career studying and teaching in the "metropolitan academy"' (Chatterjee 1993b: 64).
25. 'Postcolonial' currently stands for different kinds of struggles and includes countries that have been more recently occupied: 'The postcolonial era now involves comparable but somewhat different kinds of anti-colonial struggles in those countries more recently occupied: East Timor invaded by Indonesia when a Portuguese colony, now finally independent after a long war of resistance; Tibet by China, Taiwan by nationalist Chinese, Kashmir by India ... the Sarhaoui Democratic Arab Republic (Western Sahara) by Morocco, Palestine and the West Bank by Israel ... those First Nations seeking independence from sovereign nation states (in Canada, Ethiopia, New Zealand, USA) or by indigenous peoples in border territories seeking independence (the Kurds, the Tamils, the Uyghur), or those

suffering from the decisions of decolonization who seek union with an adjacent decolonized state (the Catholic minority in Northern Ireland who wish to join a united Ireland), or those tribal peoples who seek nothing more than their own survival, or those who were forcibly transported under colonial occupation, many of whom wish to but cannot return to their own country (the Koreans in Japan), or those fourth-world nations who seek the basic rights of legal and social equality (native Americans, the Aboriginal peoples of Australia, the so-called denotified tribes in India, the hill tribes in Bangladesh, the Ainu in Japan), or those suffering from the social stigma of caste exclusion (the Untouchables in India, the Burakumin in Japan), or disadvantaged ethnic minorities and impoverished classes in most countries of the world' (Young 2001: 3–4).

26. Most critics of postcolonial theory seem to find easy targets in Bhabha and Spivak largely because their theories underscore the presence of interstitial spaces in identity formation and owing to the obscurity of the language they use. Perhaps the critics' obsessive antagonism towards Bhabha and Spivak stems from the number of books on postcolonial theory in the last decade that have devoted chapters to both, virtually treating them as prophets of the discipline. See, for example, Young, who was the first to include chapter-length studies of Spivak and Bhabha in *White Mythologies* (1992). Moore-Gilbert's *Postcolonial Theory* (1997) and Childs and Williams's, *An Introduction to Post-Colonial Theory* (1997) followed suit.
27. As Bartolovich argues, Marxist theories are plagued with a 'curious divided consciousness'. They are '"internationalist" in political commitment, but utterly "national," if not nationalist, in the production of academic work.' For example, E. P. Thompson's insular *The Making of the English Working Class* does not consider even colonialism as a factor having any bearing upon Britain's working class (Bartolovich 2000: 143–4).
28. While cultural imagination is extremely significant in anti-colonial struggles, it must work side by side with mass mobilization which is the primary requirement in the establishment of an independent nation-state. The emerging nation-state, consequently, witnesses rapid appropriation of workers, peasants, minorities and the lower orders, and enlists their participation. But often we discover that although we have a political nation-state, the nation itself is yet to be born. In the decolonized nation, inequalities persist between the privileged and the subaltern, and indicate the widening rift between the rhetoric of nationalism and the field of political action even though nationalist ideology tends to cover up its differences. Nationalism is not a homogeneous category, but as espoused by the

intelligentsia, includes all the connotations of a popular bourgeois ideology (see Sethi 1999: 5).

29. For example, despite the multipolar nature of former President Luiz Lula da Silva's socialist policies in Brazil, São Paulo maintains two class divisions between people. The upper-class rich prefer not to mingle with the lower-class poor. The former use helicopters (the city has 250 heliports) as a mode of transport which keeps them at a fair elevation from the ordinary people in the streets below (Žižek 2009: 5).
30. This, feels Lazarus, defines Said's work on Palestinian identity, *After the Last Sky*, though Said's political urgency is largely dissipated by Bhabha's analysis of it (Lazarus 1997: 44–5). For more on Lazarus, see Chapter 2.
31. Young's definition in *Interventions*, a journal of postcolonial studies dedicated to understanding the implications of postcolonialism today, covers most aspects: 'Postcolonialism has come to name a certain kind of interdisciplinary political, theoretical and historical academic work that sets out to serve as a transnational forum of studies grounded in the historical context of colonialism, as well as in the political context of contemporary problems of globalization' (Young 1998: 4).

Chapter Two

1. See, for instance, Miyoshi (2000), Sardar and Davies (2002) and Johnson (2004).
2. Miyoshi refers to the erstwhile colony as an 'old disrupted site' that has to 'renegotiate the conditions of a nation-state in which [its residents are] to reside thereafter' (Miyoshi 2000: 1869).
3. Since the nineteenth century, nation-states in the west had accepted the inflows of capital and reoriented 'territorial politics towards the requirements of the capitalist logic' (Harvey 2003: 44), resulting in an aggressive patriotic and racist policy that would protect imperialist ventures into the state. The aggressive build-up of colonies and the creation of narrow nationalisms has been the consequence of surplus capital.
4. Transnational corporations can be distinguished from multinational corporations although the two terms are often used interchangeably. Customarily, multinational corporations are transformed into transnational corporations as simple export/import activity in local markets expands overseas. Gradually, the corporation becomes 'denationalized' as its offices and destinations, shareholders and personnel, also move out of the country of origin, leading to a sense

of loyalty only to itself. By and by, it becomes truly international in that its strength and capital are no longer a mark of the buoyancy of the country in which it first set itself up. As Miyoshi explains: '[A] multinational corporation (MNC) is one that is headquartered in a nation, operating in a number of countries. Its high-echelon personnel largely consists of the nationals of the country of origin, and the corporate loyalty is, though increasingly autonomous, finally tied to the home nation. A truly transnational corporation, on the other hand, might no longer be tied to its nation of origin but is adrift and mobile, ready to settle anywhere and exploit any state including its own, as long as the affiliation serves its own interest' (Miyoshi 2000: 1875).

5. None of these associations have been particularly successful in keeping the IMF, the WTO or the World Bank at arm's length.
6. By the year 2000, 51 of the world's most robust economies were not nations or countries, but multinational corporations (Marable 2003: 7).
7. Films today cater to a world audience since there is no audience for 'regionality'. Even regional-language films (for example those from India) can appear to be made in Hollywood – one need only press the 'mute' button. Films that were bona fide representations of national cultures such as Mehboob Khan's *Mother India* (1957), adapted from Katherine Mayo's novel (1927), now remain subjects of study only. Though the film celebrates the virtues of the Indian woman who is resurrected repeatedly in homogeneous configurations of goddesses and mothers, and has been subjected to criticism for this reason, it is nonetheless a representative film especially as its release coincided with India's new found freedom, at a time when rapid appropriation of 'national' identity was taking place (Sinha 2006: 36).

   Another outward manifestation of one's specific identity is clothing. The traditional dress in which age-old crafts like weaving and embroidery played a part is now considered outdated, having been replaced by the familiar jeans and T-shirt. Yet, ironically, the 'national' is protected and carefully marketed by commercial preservationists in upmarket and fashionable shopping areas such as the Hauz Khas village in the heart of cosmopolitan Delhi, an 'authentic' Indian village culture that Tarlo calls 'ethnic chic' (Tarlo 1996: 311).
8. One look at the aggressive Hindu websites that have enabled the global rise of the Hindu right-wing will show us that culture has become a commodity sold on plasma screens (Gopal 2003). In the US, particularly, Hindutva ideology has managed to appropriate a large section of the diaspora. It includes a Vishva Hindu Parishad

(an international forum of Hindus) of America which has its own website that promotes 'the Hindu way of life' and creates its own brand of Yankee Hindutva. A standard website contains a definition of who Hindus are and gives information about Hindu festivals and Hindu news. The websites also sell 'Puja [worship] Packages' for the 'beginner' and 'Advanced Packages' for the 'repeat visitor' (Gopal 2003: 174). One may even 'order' proxy *pujas* and *havans* (sacred fire ritual of the Hindus) online which can be performed for the non-resident Hindu in an Indian temple of his or her choice. Thus the US-Indian can enjoy the spiritual bliss of the homeland even as he/she grooves materially into the west and so reaps the benefits of 'dual' citizenship (Gopal 2003: 175–6).

9. For Ahmad, the 'structural dialectic of imperialism *includes* ... the deepening penetration of all available global spaces by the working of capital and intensification of the nation-state form simultaneously. This dialectic produces contradictory effects in realms of culture and ideology. The same Arab magnates and Irani mullahs who chase petrodollars across the globe – those same saffron yuppies who are opening up the Bombay Stock Exchange and the computer industry of Bangalore for foreign capital – organise their own lives around the fetishism of commodities bequeathed to them by advanced capital but are also the ones ... to wean [the working masses] away from the progressive projects of socialism and anti-imperialist nationalisms' (Ahmad 1995a: 12).
10. At that point, Rashmi Mayur, Director of the International Institute for Sustainable Future in Mumbai, said, arguably at the behest of the BJP: 'If we do not protect the interests of the poor peasants from the vultures of development, whose only interest is to fulfill the runaway demands of the elite and make massive profits, then our people will be obliterated and many developing societies and their cultures will be wiped out' (see Raschka 1995: n.p.).
11. The role of the nation-state in ushering in globalization has been severely criticized. As a revolutionary article attributed to 'Subcomandante Marcos' puts it: 'In the cabaret of globalization, the state gives itself over to a strip-tease, at the end of which it retains only the bare minimum: its repressive force. Its material base destroyed, its sovereignty and its independence annulled, its political class effaced, the nation-state becomes a simple security apparatus in the service of "megabusiness". Instead of targeting public investment on social spending, it prefers to improve the equipment that facilitates social control' (Marcos 1997: 566–7).
12. Arundhati Roy, a significant dissident voice from South Asia, has written and lectured extensively on the failure of democracy, the

future of progressive movements, and the unilateral American dominance of world politics. As she says: 'Earth, forest, water, air. These are the assets that the state holds in trust for the people it represents ... To snatch these away and sell them as stock to private companies is a process of barbaric dispossession on a scale that has no parallel in history' (Roy 2001: 43).

13. Dirlik echoes the same sentiment when he writes: 'The situation created by global capitalism helps explain certain phenomena that have become apparent over the last two decades, but especially since the eighties: global motions of peoples (and, therefore, cultures), the weakening of boundaries (among societies, as well as among social categories), the replication in societies internally of inequalities and discrepancies once associated with colonial differences ... Some of these phenomena have also contributed to an appearance of equalization within and among societies' (Dirlik 1994: 351).
14. Ahmad distinguishes himself sharply from such critics, placing his faith in Marxism rather than poststructuralism, when he writes: 'Since nationalism had been designated during this phase [the late 1970s] as the determinate source of ideological energy in the Third World by those same critics who had themselves been influenced mainly by poststructuralism, the disillusionment with the (national-bourgeois) state of the said Third World which began to set in towards the later 1980s then led those avant-garde theorists to declare that poststructuralism and deconstruction were the determinate positions for the critique of nationalism itself' (Ahmad 1993: 68).
15. I am indebted to Chrisman (2004) for this part of my discussion.
16. On cultural nationalism, see Smith (1991: 71–98); Plamenatz (1976: 24–7); Berlin (1976); Kohn (1944: 351–2, 381); Hutchinson and Smith (1994: 122–31); Eriksen (1993: 99–104); and in particular Kedourie (1970: 93).
17. Women's activism played a significant role in the Indian national struggle, for example. Women's organizations like Desh Sevika Sangh, the Nari Satyagraha Samiti, the Mahila Rashtriya Sangh, the Swayam Sevika Sangh and many others were set up, even though the national movement is regarded as patriarchal in nature (Kumar 1993: 79). Women were to reject foreign goods, support the production of cottage industries, especially spinning and weaving *khadi* (or home spun), hold meetings and demonstrations and preach the advantages of liberty and freedom. Apart from these symbolic activities, women had also become well entrenched in the Communist Party and were participants in demands to own property, and for education and voting rights.

18. Fanon also advocates, above all, social and political consciousness among the people, following decolonization. Mere national consciousness awakened by the bourgeoisie leadership will not do: 'What we want to hear about are the experiments carried out by the Argentinians or the Burmese in their efforts to overcome illiteracy or the dictatorial tendencies of their leaders. It is these things which strengthen us, teach us and increase our efficiency ten times over. As we see it, a programme is necessary for a government which really wants to free the people politically and socially. There must be an economic programme; there must also be a doctrine concerning the division of wealth and social relations' (Fanon 1967: 164). In a similar vein, Amilcar Cabral has pointed out: 'We take pride in the fact that thousands of adults have been taught to read and write, that the rural inhabitants are receiving medicines that were never available to them before ... This is the greatest victory of the people of Guinea and Cape Verde over the Portuguese colonialists' (cited in Chrisman 2004: 196–7). But despite Cabral, Guinea-Bissau today is one of the world's poorest nations owing mainly to the 1998–99 civil war. It owes the US more than $900 million and thus follows a Structural Adjustment Programme imposed upon it by the IMF.
19. While nationalism is faulted for being a borrowed western form, Rabindranath Tagore, an Indian nationalist poet, advocated a belief in dismissing national boundaries and political freedom altogether as a cure for the world's problems (Tagore 1918: 97–130). So detached is Tagore's ideal of universalism from the ideology of human liberation that *swaraj*, or home rule, becomes no more than *maya*, 'a mist that will vanish, leaving no strain on the radiance of the Eternal' (Tagore 2002: 103). His thoughts find realization in his popular novel *Gora* where a juxtaposition of nationalist ideals and contemporary politics is shown to 'violate' the 'fundamental principles of Indianness and Hinduism' (Nandy 1994: 40).
20. Other campaigns that were 'national' even though they predate the Indian national movement by almost a hundred years (and are thereby not associated with the national uprising) include the Indigo Revolt of 1859–60 in Bengal, which resulted from years of coercive indigo farming. The Indigo Revolt involved strikes and disturbances by hundreds of villagers who refused to pay high rents and grow indigo which brought no fruitful returns. This initiative would have failed were it not for the pronounced organizational and disciplinary nature of the uprising, which was marked by a complete unity among Hindu and Muslim peasants regardless of any antipathy on the grounds of religion or caste. There was no 'fake', essentialistic 'Indian' identity based on a Hindu ethnic core

culture which mobilized these peasants. Other peasant rebellions include the Pabna revolt in 1873 and the agrarian outbreaks in Poona and Ahmednagar in 1875, which pertained largely to the abolition of illegal coercive methods such as forced eviction and the seizure of crops and cattle. What is striking about peasant insurgency in these cases is their convergence on the basic demand for the removal of immediate injustices and the protection of their fundamental rights through the legal state apparatus. Large causes like national liberation and anti-imperialist demands were not part of their objective: these uprisings were neither aimed at the system of *zamindari* or landlordship, nor did they have at any juncture a slant against imperialism (Chandra et al. 1989: 50–60.) The peasants raised no anti-British demands; in fact they used the legal system to oppose their immediate landlords. At no stage did the agrarian leaders have anything to do with the British; in fact, the peasants asserted their loyalty to Britain by desiring 'to be the *ryots* [peasants] of Her Majesty the Queen and of Her only' (Chandra et al. 1989: 55). Considering that the *zamindars* were, in effect, agents of the British and appointed by them, the willingness of the peasants to be of service to the Queen reveals both their ignorance of colonial implications and the limited nature of their nationalism. Again, in so far as the Hindu–Muslim issue was concerned, the peasants showed complete unity in spite of the statistical balance being in favour of the Muslim peasants, though the *zamindars* were largely Hindu.

Another instance of conflict between the peasants and the moneylenders, in the Deccan (the Sirur *taluq*), arose not from national sentiment emerging from the evils of colonization but from the practices of coercive moneylenders who compelled the peasants to surrender their land when they were unable to pay land revenue. The Sirur disturbances soon instigated rebellion in other villages – Poona, Ahmednagar, Sholapur and Satara – where peasants looted and burnt moneylenders' houses and shops for the main purpose of destroying official records containing promissory notes or contracts signed under pressure. That the peasants were hardly motivated by national causes is evident from the marked serenity which followed the agitation, assisted by the Deccan Agriculturists' Relief Act of 1879 which vastly reduced dependence on moneylenders. The colonial government thus appears to have been sympathetic to the peasants since the immediate aggression was that of the oppressive *zamindars* (Chandra et al. 1989: 58).

What needs to be emphasized in these accounts is the modest nature of peasant rebellion and the imperfect understanding of colonialism by the peasantry. The uprisings existed only at the level of peasant problems without resentment of colonial rule. The peasants were not acutely aware of the social and political forces behind the movements themselves, even though these accounts became part of the nation's history in the twentieth century, with the efforts of the modern intelligentsia to appropriate peasant discontentment for the national movement.

21. In 'Signs Taken for Wonders', Bhabha writes in favour of utter ambiguity: 'If the effect of colonial power is seen to be the production of hybridization rather than the noisy command of colonialist authority or the silent repression of native traditions, then an important change of perspective occurs. The ambivalence at the source of traditional discourses on authority enables a form of subversion, founded on the undecidability that turns the discursive conditions of dominance into the grounds of intervention' (Bhabha 1994: 112).
22. Lazarus and Bartolovich criticize Gilroy's *The Black Atlantic* (1993) for refusing to take on board world-system theories in the production of modernity. In dismissing the distinctions between core and periphery, Gilroy argues that no culture can exist so neatly: the cultures of indentured labour, enslaved blacks and exterminated 'Indians' commingle increasingly with those of imperialists and European settlers. Hence, the discourse of the nation-state as an empowering and liberating force is insular and parochial. Bartolovich insists that although cultures cannot be sealed off 'hermetically', 'they certainly *are* sealed off politically' (Bartolovich 2000: 139). As such, Gilroy's views about the absolutism of nations are 'disabling in the context of "anticolonial war", where a unified front against a distinct oppressive power is needed, and a distinct insurgent "culture" is born out of that struggle' (Bartolovich 2000: 139–40). For Lazarus, Gilroy's prioritizing of black slaves as the bearers of modernity ignores 'the vast and collective historical experiences – of indenture, wage labour, forced migration, colonization, etc. – that subtended and existed alongside slavery and that are as inextricably constitutive of the modern world as slavery is' (Lazarus 1999: 63). The exclusion of experiences connected with historical materialism in the theorization of modernity, which is global in its reach, and within which the rise of the nation-state plays an imperative role, is, for Lazarus, Gilroy's chief deficiency.
23. That may be the only way in which the narrative of the nation can be 'plotted' if it has to mediate between 'the teleology of progress' and 'the "timeless" discourse of irrationality' (Bhabha 1990b: 294).
24. The markets want states to remain impotent so that they can exercise their 'vested interests'. At the same time, the complete fragmentation

of the state is not a desired end since the global capitalist system is predicated upon the organization of the nation-states: the states must '*remain states*' (Bauman 1998: 68). Bauman writes very candidly that weak states have to be kept as such so that they can 'act with the consent of global capital' and desist from slowing down the mechanism of capital inflows: 'Throwing wide open the gates and abandoning any thought of autonomous economic policy is the preliminary, and meekly complied with, condition of eligibility for financial assistance from world banks and monetary funds' (Bauman 1998: 68).

25. Susan Strange believes it to be yet another example of eurocentrism to declare that nation-states are declining. Not just in the old Soviet Union, people are clamoring for their own states in Canada, Australia, India and Africa. The Kurds, the Basques, the Scots and the Corsicans also want their own state but are as yet not vociferous enough in their agitation (Strange 2004: 220).
26. See 'Disinvestment and Privatisation', available at http://dpe.nic.in/survey0506/vol1/vol1ch6.pdf
27. The Bolivarian Alliance comprises of Latin American countries like Bolivia, Cuba, Ecuador, Honduras, Nicaragua, Venezuela, Antigua and Barbuda, St Vincent, the Grenadines and Dominica. Hugo Chávez, in his efforts to help the poor and the excluded (which his critics call populism) has rejected US foreign policy in favour of a 'multipolar' world in which each citizen has the right to a dignified life (see Llana 2009: n.p.).

Chapter Three

1. Miyoshi is not off the mark when he writes: 'By allowing ourselves to get absorbed into the discourse on "postcoloniality" or even post-Marxism, we are fully collaborating with the hegemonic ideology which looks, as usual, as if it were not ideology at all' (Miyoshi 2000: 1886).
2. Nehru relied far more on the 'rule-bound incompetence' of his bureaucracy than on his party during the first decade of India's independence (Khilnani 1997: 38).
3. See 'The Pitfalls of National Consciousness' in Fanon (1967: 120, 165). Fanon distinguishes very clearly between national consciousness and social and political consciousness: 'National consciousness, instead of being the all-embracing crystallization of the innermost hopes of the whole people, instead of being the immediate and most obvious result of the mobilization of the people, will be in any case only an empty shell, a crude and fragile

travesty of what it might have been. The faults that we find in it are quite sufficient explanation of the facility with which, when dealing with young and independent nations, the nation is passed over for the race, and the tribe is preferred to the state. These are the cracks in the edifice which show the process of retrogression that is so harmful and prejudicial to national effort and national unity' (119). A bourgeoisie that can offer only nationalism for its people 'fails in its mission and gets caught up in a whole series of mishaps'. Unless nationalism is 'enriched and deepened by a very rapid transformation into a consciousness of social and political needs, in other words into humanism, it leads up a blind alley' (165).

4. Sachs's programme for the upliftment of the economy came to be known later as 'shock therapy' since it included the employment of all the 'principles' of globalization such as increased privatization, trade liberalization and reduced subsidies to restrict hyperinflation.
5. Russia even surrendered its robust scientific research policies, forcing its top scientists to take their talents westward. Just before the 1991 collapse, the USSR had one third of the world's engineers and one quarter of its physicists (Aronowitz 2003: 192).
6. It is imperative to separate domestic prices from world prices so that billions of farmers in the developing world find a way of surviving. In his detailed study of Egyptian and Chinese farming practices, Amin insists that agrobusiness must not be allowed unchecked into countries following non-capitalist agricultural practices (Amin 2004: 226–7).
7. All the time, countries undergoing SAPs believe themselves to be free and sovereign: 'For France has never stopped being there, advising African leaders and suggesting to them which policies they should implement. For decades now we have been living in a neocolonial situation, while passing for independent countries' (Notes 2003: 39).
8. Galeano holds the policies of the United States responsible for the steady downscaling of the Latin American economy. A detailed account of the financial mess Latin American countries are in today is the subject of *Open Veins of Latin America* where he writes: '[T]oday's imperialism radiates technology and progress, and even the use of this old, unpleasant word to define it is in bad taste. But when imperialism begins exalting its own virtues we should take a look in our pockets. We find that the new model does not make its colonies more prosperous, although it enriches their poles of development; it does not ease social and religious tensions, but aggravates them; it spreads poverty even more widely and concentrates wealth even more narrowly; ... it takes over the

internal market and the mainsprings of the productive apparatus; it assumes proprietary rights to chart the course and fix the frontiers of progress; ... it denationalizes not only industry but the profits earned by industry; ... it does not bring in capital for development but takes it out' (Galeano 1997: 207).

9. In Indonesia, the bloody coup staged by General Suharto was aided by the US and Britain because he had agreed to reinstate several western companies and the World Bank once in power.
10. The WTO treaty, which was signed in Marrakesh, Morocco, contains 22,000 pages which could not possibly have been read by the 120 member countries who were its signatories.
11. As Friedrich List wrote in 1856: 'It is a vulgar rule of prudence for him who has reached the pinnacle of power to cast down the ladder by which he mounted, that others may not follow ... A nation which by protective duties and maritime restrictions has built up a manufacturing industry and a merchant marine to such a point of strength and power as not to fear the competition of any other, can pursue no safer policy than to thrust aside the means of elevation to preach to other nations the advantages of free trade, and to utter loud expressions of repentance for having walked hitherto in the way of error, and for having come so lately to the knowledge of truth' (List 1856: 440).
12. The growing margin between the rich and the poor was well evinced in the defeat of the BJP party in the 2004 general elections in India where the party slogan 'India Shining' was based exclusively on the rising sensitive index at the stock exchange and the steady growth of the country's GDP. But the routing of the BJP exposed the underside of globalization in the deteriorating condition of the Indian poor. In Latin America too, 'progress' and 'national liberation' have become sheer rhetoric within the inflexibility of a global capitalist network manipulated by big US corporations. And even though there has been an increased demand for local products resulting from globalization, it has had no effect on the expansion of the mass market. The only effects are an abysmal decline in the purchasing power and an unprecedented growth of prices, and significantly, the destruction of trade unions.
13. In spite of the feeble efforts of the United Nations, Israel refuses to tear down the construction of the barrier in the West Bank. In 2004, when the World Court was urged by members of the General Assembly of the UN to advise the prime minister, Ariel Sharon, to dismantle the barrier, his senior adviser Raanan Gissin stated unequivocally: 'The building of the fence will go on.' He called the UN vote a 'tyranny of the majority' (Reuters 2004: 18). Notably,

the United States voted against the resolution in a 150 to 6 vote (see also Klein 2002a: xxii). Examples from history include the Great Wall of China, the Berlin Wall and Hadrian's Wall (built by the Roman emperor, Hadrian, in AD 122 to separate England and Wales, which were under his command, from Scotland).

14. While financial institutions in the west deter developing economies from exercising precautions against the persuasions of globalization, the US robustly supports its own banks and corporations in financial crises through 'socialist' measures. During the 2008 financial meltdown, for instance, the United States used all the appropriate measures to protect its institutions from bankruptcy, while maintaining the illusion of growth. The US countered the 2008 recession by giving bail-out packages to big banks, which Žižek calls 'the robbery of the century' (Žižek 2009: 12). He asks: 'Is the bail-out plan really a "socialist" measure then, the birth of state socialism in the US? If it is, it is a very peculiar form: a "socialist" measure whose primary aim is not to help the poor, but the rich, not those who borrow, but those who lend. In a supreme irony, "socializing" the banking system is acceptable when it serves to save capitalism' (13).

    In his recent book, *Freefall*, Stiglitz evokes the same disillusionment with US economy: 'This is not the way things were supposed to be. Modern economics, with its faith in free markets and globalization, had promised prosperity for all. The much-touted New Economy – the amazing innovations that marked the latter half of the twentieth century, including deregulation and financial engineering – was supposed to enable better risk management, bringing with it the end of the business cycle. If the combination of the New Economy and modern economics had not eliminated economic fluctuations, at least it was taming them. Or so we were told' (Stiglitz 2010: xi).

15. The lack of forest cover and the degradation of the ecosystem has led to the virtual extinction of the Bengal Tiger, as tigers frequently wandering into neighbouring villages in search of food are often killed by locals.

16. Not only should greater attention be paid to the framing of economic policies to prevent the neglect of women but mainstream feminist movements should also not sever themselves off from women's grassroots problems. Debates involving the growing distance between north and south have become so dominant that feminist analyses of globalization have been substantially neglected. This is particularly true after the September 11 events when the 'clash of civilizations' thesis marginalized women altogether in view of

the discussions on fundamentalism, markets and globalization that followed. Faludi deals with this aspect in *The Terror Dream, Fear and Fantasy in Post-9/11 America* (Faludi 2007).

17. As Young has pointed out, Bhabha leaves us unsure as to whether the mutation from psychological categories of resistance to revolution happened at the level of interpretation rather than, in fact, in historical time. There would have to be a historical consciousness, however essentialized, in which Bhabha's privileged moments could be contained (Young 1992: 149–55).
18. The stories of the escapades of Robin Hood and his merry men were a folk representation meant to describe the resistance of common people to the ruling classes who had fenced off common land for sheep grazing. This rich class of industrialists believed in the beneficence of the wool industry and thus created the concept of the 'enclosure': 'These unprecedented enclosures were precursors to mass clearing of the lands of peasants, and the eventual ushering of these people into the cities to become the factory workers of the industrial revolution where their labour, too, became an "enclosed" community' (Notes 2003: 27). This led to massive privatization in England and the end of commonly held land whose ownership once belonged with the people. Correspondingly, cultures and traditions of common people underwent mutation or fell into disuse. More importantly, people who were formerly self sufficient began to rely on an economy based on cash. This is the way fencing of land works.
19. Dissent is often expressed by anti-capitalist protestors in novel ways: men and women dress up in tuxedos and evening gowns and press fake currency into the hands of policemen, or they use giant catapults to throw soft toys and confetti at the heads of state gathered inside the fencing, as they did in Quebec City in 2001.
20. As each hill-woman clung to a tree, forest officials and contractors could not go ahead with the work of sawing and chopping.
21. On this subject, see Sethi (2007: 30).
22. See Zutshi (1993: 100–1) who argues that the women's question cannot be either liberated from or resolved within nationalist accounts. See also see Radhakrishnan (1992: 77–95) for a discussion of the women's question and its ghettoization within the politics of nationalism.
23. Nayereh Tohidi also reinforces the argument that any anti-imperialist revolution which does not transform the position of third-world women is inadequate: 'Alone, a women's movement can never transform the foundations of sexism and sexual oppression. Neither can a revolution which seeks to transform class relationships

meet its goals if it does not incorporate the question of women's oppression. Specific demands of women must be incorporated into the national antiimperialist movement and class struggle right from the beginning. *The women's question should not be relegated to the days after the revolution* – as has been, unfortunately, the tendency of many left and revolutionary movements. Cases such as the Algerian and Iranian revolutions have proven that the success of a nationalist or even a socialist revolution does not automatically lead to liberation for women' (Tohidi 1991: 260).

24. Notions of female power in which the woman-nature-mother connection is exploited are the target of anti-essentialism groups who see nurturing acts within the terminology of a sexist patriarchy that can only reinforce male ideology. Such an interpretation as worked out in the context of environmental feminism might disquiet feminist readers for whom such universalisms are disempowering. It might appear (especially in first-world struggles) that 'motherhood' is an entirely apolitical act of resistance, but keeping in mind the traditional lifestyles of third-world women, the emphasis on the politicization of gendered identities is helpful in finding a common front in a society that is widely divergent, socially and economically.
25. Other global pressures come from the over-use of fossil fuel and the cutting down of trees. This has led to the unavailability of fodder and the drying up of other skills related to farming.
26. Sardar explains how '[d]uring the colonial period and under modernity, everything non-western and indigenous to traditional cultures was reviled and shunned; in postmodernism, concern for Other cultures has revived, and they are now appropriated, repackaged and marketed in the name of plurality and multiculturalism' (Sardar 1998: 124–5). Part of the appropriation comes from Roddick's claim of being 'inspired by Mahatama (*sic*) Gandhi, Martin Luther and African tribal chiefs' as though these men had contributed to the business of *The Body Shop*. Body massage in Thailand is another example of an ancient practice of remedial and therapeutic massage being repackaged for sex-starved western tourists for their ultimate sexual *nirvana* (Sardar 1998: 123–7).
27. As Vijay Jawandhia of the All India Farmers' Union says: 'Pests have become immune to pesticides, and the fertilizer has depleted the soil so we have to add more to get the same level of production' (Notes 2003: 162).
28. Swarms of men and women, calling themselves the Intercontinental Caravan of Solidarity and Resistance (ICC), created a virtual India over the German-Swiss countryside, cooking their *rotis* and making cauldrons of *chai*, some even smoking their *hookahs* with

their Aeroflot tags still hanging from them (Notes 2003: 161). On a smaller scale, another agitation worth mentioning is that of the farmers of Punjab who gather every summer in the capital, Chandigarh, to appeal to the Chief Minister to at least cover their costs of production. They convert Chandigarh's famous Rose Garden into their lodgings, bathe in its fountains and defecate in the rose bushes while the city's myopic elite curse openly. Having viewed them at close quarters, it is a little difficult to take sides with this anti-globalization brigade.

29. The demonstrations against the World Bank and the WTO are signs of resistance to the forces of the market that can come only from nationalist struggles. According to Jameson, the nationalist spirit alone can be successfully employed 'in fighting for labour protection laws against the global free-market push; in the resistance of national cultural "protectionist" policies, or the defence of patent law, against an American "universalism" that would sweep away local culture and pharmaceutical industries, along with whatever welfare safety-net and socialized medical systems might still be in place. Here, the defense of the national suddenly becomes the defense of the welfare state itself' (Jameson 2000: 66).
30. As a report published by Oxfam International says: 'Increased prosperity has gone hand in hand with mass poverty and the widening of already obscene inequalities between rich and poor. World trade has the potential to act as a powerful motor for the reduction of poverty, as well as for economic growth, but that potential is being lost. The problem is not that international trade is inherently opposed to the needs and interests of the poor, but that the rules that govern it are rigged in favour of the rich' (Oxfam 2002: 5).
31. Stiglitz advocates a 'globalization of knowledge' which implies the judicious adoption of privatization and liberalization without relying overmuch on the 'Washington Consensus' (Stiglitz 2004: 201). A knowledge of globalization includes setting aside reserves, maintaining safety nets to prevent recession, government quotas, safeguarding against biopiracy, and so on. The reason why East Asian economies profited from globalization is related to the manner in which trade liberalization was introduced. Korea and Taiwan, for example, benefited from 'globalization of knowledge', using which they efficiently regulated financial markets to their own advantage. 'While markets lie at the heart of every successful economy', writes Stiglitz, they 'do not work well on their own' (Stiglitz 2010: xii).
32. When the Bretton Woods conference took place in 1944 and set up the IMF and what later came to be called the World Bank, Lord

Keynes, who had chaired a session, declared that the event involving 44 countries would turn 'the brotherhood of man' into something 'more than a phrase' (cited in Panitch and Gindin 2004: 37).

33. But finding common ground between different groups has its own set of problems. Amin warns us that 'the authorities ... [use] all the measures at their disposal to prevent the unification of the peasant movement at the national level [making certain that it cannot] present itself as a spokesperson/actor/participant on equal footing with other sectors of society (the bourgeoisie, the urban popular classes, the authorities) in drawing up global strategies for the development of the country' (Amin 2004: 231).
34. Said had pointed out as early as *Orientalism* that 'an openly polemical and right-minded "progressive" scholarship can very easily degenerate into dogmatic slumber' (Said 1978: 327). Young has also expressed anxiety over the rapidity with which postcolonialism is becoming 'stagnated' and 'reified' in its approach mainly because 'we have stopped asking questions about the limits and boundaries of our own assumptions' (Young 1995: 164). This is not helped by the fact, as Moore-Gilbert indicates, that one of Bhabha's essays, 'The Postcolonial and the Postmodern', was published three times under three different titles in quick succession with scarcely a change, signalling an exhaustion. There is also very little textual dependence and cross-referencing between the three major critics of postcolonial theory – Said, Spivak and Bhabha (Moore-Gilbert 1997: 186–9).
35. As Arundhati Roy puts it, the areas infested with the maoist rebels should be called 'MoU-ist corridor' and not the 'Maoist corridor' (cited in Lakshman 2010: 9).
36. Gikandi's essay is premised on the sad story of two Guinean boys whose bodies were found in the cargo along with a letter addressed to the 'Excellencies, gentlemen, and responsible citizens of Europe' pleading their case of wanting to leave Africa (Gikandi 2001: 630). Gikandi confronts the narrative of globalization as a celebration of difference and hybridity with the plight of the two boys whose flight confirms the Enlightenment rationale of the binaries that postcolonialism attempts to demystify.

Chapter Four

1. See Kaplan (1993: 17) and Sharpe (2000b: 122).
2. As Dirlik writes: 'It is a ... reflection on the ideology of post-colonialism that, with rare exceptions ... postcolonial critics have been silent on the relationship of the idea of postcolonialism to its

context in contemporary capitalism; indeed, they have suppressed the necessity of considering such a possible relationship by repudiating a foundational role to capitalism in history' (Dirlik 1994: 331).

3. And yet, Lawrence Buell, citing Fernández Retamar, claims Caliban as America's own because he 'appears to have been associated with Yankeedom before Latin Americans thought to canonize him' (Buell 1992: 421).
4. Sharpe vehemently dissociates the term 'postcolonial' from the trajectory of US history as it 'does not fully capture the history of a white settler colony that appropriated land from Native Americans, incorporated parts of Mexico, and imported slaves and indentured labor from Africa and Asia and whose foreign policy in East Asia, the Philippines, Latin America, and the Caribbean accounts, in part, for its new immigrants' (Sharpe 2000a: 106).
5. See Glasberg (2000: 156).
6. In many ways, the United States shows itself to be a 'reluctant imperialist' (Kaplan 2004: 4). Kaplan borrows this expression from Sebastian Mallaby to connote a sentiment similar in meaning to the 'white man's burden' by which the US takes on the role of a policeman unwillingly because there is simply too much terrorism in the world and not many who can save the world from anarchy.
7. Kapur (1990: 56) has made use of the term 'tradition-in-use' to refer to the use of the repository of past traditions. She calls tradition a mobile signifier, something that changes with time and need. What lies beneath tradition-in-use is an ideal and what motivates such usage is convenience (see also Said 1993: xiv–v).
8. See Buell (1996: 88) for the distinction he makes between 'America' and the 'United States'.
9. See also Stratton (2000: 54) for an interpretation of the 'postcolonial imaginary'.
10. Haiti also manufactures baseballs even though no one plays baseball in Haiti (Galeano 1997: 275).
11. In 1904, Theodore Roosevelt had echoed the same sentiment about America's 'world duty': 'A great free people owes to itself and to all mankind not to sink into helplessness before the powers of evil' (cited in Panitch and Gindin 2004: 29).
12. The appellation 'rogue state' is assigned by the US to countries like Libya, Afghanistan, Iran, North Korea and especially Iraq for unleashing terror and despoiling world peace. For Chomsky, powerful countries like the US itself are suitable candidates for this title (see Chomsky 2000: 30).

13. But US financial hegemony has not been a complete success story. Clearly, Malaysia was not content playing yes-man and chose to opt out of the consensus by resisting the operations of the IMF and restoring capital controls over the economy. This led Friedman to write: 'Ah, excuse me, Mahathir, but what planet are you living on? You talk about participating in globalization as if it were a choice you had. Globalization isn't a choice. It's a reality ... And the most basic truth about globalization is this: *No one is in charge* ... We all want to believe that someone is in charge and responsible. But the global marketplace today is an Electronic Herd of often anonymous stock, bond, and currency traders and multinational investors, connected by screens and networks' (Friedman 2000: 112–13). Despite Friedman's claim, during the World Trade Organization summit in Seattle, a handful of non-governmental organizations were able to pinpoint the individuals and institutions that were plotting the collapse of the Asian markets, not to speak of the anti-globalization protests that marked the event. The isolation of the US in the future will, no doubt, enable everybody to face the fact of US imperialism.
14. In his speech at the National Defense University, Washington DC, President Obama declared loftily: 'Now make no mistake, this nation will maintain our military dominance. We will have the strongest armed forces in the history of the world' (Ditz 2009: n.p.). In defence expenditure, Obama has curtailed spending to the tune of a mere $8.8 billion and cancelled the purchase of F-22 fighter aircraft (Johnson 2009: n.p.). But in the year to come, it is estimated that even more money will be pumped into the Pentagon budget than was sanctioned by Bush.
15. Said's *Orientalism* accomplished this task like no other work of scholarship.
16. See Schueller and Watts (2003: 7).
17. Prominent among them are King's *Postcolonial America* and Singh and Schmidt's *Postcolonial Theory and the United States*.
18. Buell attempts to examine 'the extent to which the emergence of a flourishing national literature during the so-called Renaissance period of the mid-nineteenth century can be brought into focus through the lens of more recent post-colonial literatures' (Buell 1992: 411). In Kaplan's words, Buell 'colonizes postcolonial theory by implicitly positing the United States as the original postcolonial nation' (Kaplan 1993: 21).
19. It comes as no surprise when Ahmad writes: 'The "post" in post-colonialism signified ... the moment of a fundamental rupture that came with decolonization and therefore led to equally fundamental

but also equally determinate rearticulations in the alignment of class forces and state apparatuses ... It has now become quite common to push the moment of postcolonialism back to the American Revolution, the decolonization of Latin America, the founding of Australia; indeed, according to some, postcolonialism begins with colonialism itself, with the earliest practices of resistance, perhaps as early as 1492' (Ahmad 1995b: 14).

20. See, in this respect, Pease (1994).
21. So marked are the debates on hybridity that many books on the issue have been published. Werbner and Madood's *Debating Cultural Hybridity* (1997) is an example of this genre.
22. If, on the one hand, Rowe attempts to keep the imperialist agendas of the US presumably in check through the new American Studies, he also uses first-person plurals to suggest his endorsement of the Gulf War. Surprisingly, in the same essay, while exhorting that the new American Studies should be 'inclusive and diverse', he writes: '[W]hat separates cultural understanding from cultural imperialism is increasingly difficult to articulate in an age of technologically accelerated human and cultural mobility' (Rowe 2002b: 171).
23. In a recent essay, Arundhati Roy poses the question: 'Is there life after democracy?' which implies that 'the system of representative democracy – too much representation, too little democracy – needs some structural adjustment' (Roy 2009: ix–x). In like manner, Henry Giroux writes: 'Under the rubric of common sense, democracy is now used to invoke rationalizations for invading other countries, bailing out the rich and sanctioning the emergence of a national security state that increasingly criminalizes the social relations and behaviors that characterize those most excluded from what might be called the consumer- and celebrity-laden dreamworlds of a market-driven society. As democracy is removed from relations of equality, justice and freedom, it undergoes a legitimation crisis as it is transformed from a mode of politics that subverts authoritarian tendencies to one that reproduces them. Used to gift wrap the interests and values of an authoritarian culture, the rhetoric of democracy is now invoked to legitimate its opposite, a discourse of security and a culture of fear enlisted by pundits and other anti-public intellectuals as all-embracing registers for mobilizing a rampant nationalism, hatred of immigrants and a bunker politics organized around an "us" versus "them" mentality' (Giroux 2010: n.p.).
24. In this respect, also see Edwards (2003: 81): 'The danger of bringing a globalized American Studies into the postcolonial studies conversation is that the latter will be colonized by the former, in a way that mirrors the neocolonial apparatus of U.S. empire and that

will further limit attention to local languages and peripheral cultural formations that challenge the nation form buttressed silently within globalization.'

25. As argued in the introductory chapter, Ahmad firmly indicts third-world intellectuals who have migrated to western institutions, a move he associates with expediency encouraged by greater capital flows: 'What we have witnessed, however, is that the combination of class origin, professional ambition and lack of a prior political grounding in a stable socialist praxis predisposes a great many of the radicalized immigrants located in the metropolitan university towards both an opportunistic kind of Third-Worldism as the appropriate form of oppositional politics and a kind of self-censoring, which in turn impels them towards greater incorporation in modes of politics and discourse already authorized by the prevailing fashion in that university' (Ahmad 1993: 86).
26. As McClintock sums up polemically: 'By what fiat of historical amnesia can the United States of America, in particular, qualify as "post-colonial" – a term which can only be a monumental affront to the Native American peoples who opposed the confetti triumphalism of 1992?' (McClintock 1993: 294). Not to speak of aboriginal displacement, most of the states of America were either the trophies of war or purchased. Florida, for instance, was purchased from Spain in 1819, Alaska from Russia in 1867, and Louisiana from France in 1803 (Young 2001: 3). Yet many call downtown Los Angeles the real capital of the postcolonial 'Third World' (San Juan 1998: 4).

CHAPTER FIVE

1. Such rifts, for instance, were seen frequently between the current United Progressive Alliance government and its left supporters in India prior to the parliamentary elections of 2009. This resulted in conflict between the forces of the market place and of labour, between the corporate world and the conservationists. Prior to 2004, when the BJP government in India was in power, conflicts between the left and the party in power occurred frequently over issues of privatization and foreign direct investment.
2. Parry proclaims that 'the most elaborate obituary of proletarian internationalism is to be found in *Empire*' (Parry 2004b: 96).
3. Interestingly, Brecher refers to the protests of the anti-globalization demonstrators in Seattle as the 'Battle of Seattle' (Brecher 2003: 203).

4. *Empire* concludes by advocating a three-fold programme for the global multitude – 'global citizenship', 'a social wage and guaranteed income for all', and 'the right to reappropriation' (Hardt and Negri 2000: 400–6). The second demand may be the only concrete political programme envisaged by the writers, the first and the third being ambiguous and vague (see Callinicos 2003: 136). The desire for guaranteed wages is a long-standing wish of left politics.
5. Hardt states, on the contrary, that '[p]olitical struggle in the age of network movements no longer works that way. Despite the apparent strength of those who occupied centre stage and dominated the representations of the Forum [Porto Alegre], they may ultimately prove to have lost the struggle' (Hardt 2002: 117).
6. In this connection, Eduardo Galeano writes: 'In the rigid framework of a global capitalism integrated around the big U.S. corporations, the industrialization of Latin America has increasingly less to do with progress and national liberation. The talisman was robbed of its power in the decisive defeats of the past century, when ports triumphed over interiors and free trade crushed new-born national industries' (Galeano 1997: 208).
7. Other than defying the Kyoto protocol, the US has been responsible for wriggling out of international policies concerning efforts to restrain biological weapons and nuclear proliferation. Its other unilateral procedures include its lack of support for the establishment of an international war crimes tribunal or for the Anti-Ballistic Missile Treaty. The US supports its own interests, as when championing its steel industry, while urging other countries to impose austerity measures on their public spending. The US is also the stingiest in offering aid: the richest nation in the world offered to pay a sum of only $250,000 for the World Conference Against Racism as compared with $10 million offered by the Ford Foundation.
8. In *Baghdad Burning*, originally the blog of a young Iraqi girl, now published as a book, Riverbend (a pseudonym) describes the lives of her family and friends amidst bomb and missile attacks and the overall destruction of Iraq's infrastructure and civil society. She recounts the terror of waiting for a bomb to explode any moment and lists why and when she hated American troops the most – as when they opened fire on school children and their parents in Fallujah, or when they humiliated her by searching her family's car and belongings, or when they shot her friend's family as they were preparing to evacuate their house to leave for a safe place. Riverbend is almost frightened of her new-found talent for being

able to distinguish the sound of a pistol from that of a machine-gun, a tank from an armoured vehicle (Riverbend 2006: 11–12, 14–15).

9. Post-9/11 television coverage in the US did not contain any discussion of the reasons behind the violence (Brah 2002: 39). When Afghanistan became the prime target of the American media, and even later when Iraq replaced it, there were scarcely any voices of disapproval or opposition on national television. On the other hand, high-pitched rhetoric about civilizational values versus barbarism echoed the polarities of nineteenth-century colonial discourse. This was lent support by the spectacle of an Afghani woman, the subject of a British documentary film, being shot by bullets in a sports complex in Afghanistan that was shown repeatedly on American TV. The documentary was called 'Beneath the Veil', as if to demonstrate the subterranean civilizational aberrations that differentiate east from west (Brah 2002: 39). Brah writes that the Afghan woman was portrayed in a manner that 'leaves little scope for the articulation of Afghani female agency, such that by the time we get to the actual scene of the woman being killed, it becomes extremely difficult to dissociate this merciless and deplorable act from the long-standing western representational regime of the "barbaric other" in general and the "barbaric Muslim" in particular' (Brah 2002: 40).
10. As Harvey warns: 'The danger ... [lies in] seeing all such struggles against dispossession as by definition "progressive" or, even worse, of placing them under some homogenizing banner like that of [the] "multitude"' (Harvey 2003: 169). Resistance must be wary of homogeneity and at the same time avoid particularism: 'Some way must be found, both theoretically and politically, to move beyond the amorphous concept of "the multitude" without falling into the trap of "my community, locality, or social group right or wrong"' (Harvey 2003: 179). If movements against globalization can distinguish between its positive and negative aspects and widen their own local platforms, reasonable gains can be attained that may not be possible by always emphasizing localism.
11. In this respect, see Hall (1991; 1990).
12. Towards the end of the book, Said warns against 'the fact of consumerism in the Orient': 'No one needs to be reminded that oil, the region's greatest resource, has been totally absorbed into the United States economy ... My point is that the relationship is a one-sided one, with the United States a selective customer of a very few products (oil and cheap manpower mainly), the Arabs highly diversified consumers of a vast range of United States products, material and ideological' (Said 1978: 324). Said goes on to write of a 'vast standardization of taste' reflected in the consumerization

of blue jeans and Coca-Cola, and startlingly about 'cultural images of the Orient supplied by American mass media and consumed unthinkingly by the mass television audience' (Said 1978: 324–5). The US invasions of Afghanistan and Iraq and the television images so generated reflect the latter perfectly.

13. See, for instance, Spivak (1989: 276; 1992: 9–18).

BIBLIOGRAPHY

Abu-Lughod, Janet (1991) 'Going Beyond the Global Babble'. *Culture, Globalization and the World-System*. Ed. Anthony D. King (Hampshire and London: Macmillan): 131–7.

Adam, Barbara (2002) 'The Gendered Time Politics of Globalization: Of Shadowlands and Elusive Justice'. *Feminist Review*, Vol. 70: 3–29.

Ahmad, Aijaz (1993) *In Theory: Classes, Nations, Literatures* (New Delhi: Oxford University Press).

——. (1995a) 'The Politics of Literary Postcoloniality', *Race and Class*, Vol. 36, No. 3: 1–20.

——. (1995b) 'Postcolonialism: What's in a Name?' *Late Imperial Culture*. Eds Román de la Campa, E. Ann Kaplan and Michael Sprinker (London and New York: Verso): 11–32.

Alagranati, Claro, José Seoane and Emilio Taddei (2004) 'Neoliberalism and Social Conflict: The Popular Movements in Latin America'. *Globalizing Resistance: The State of Struggle*. Eds François Polet and CETRI (London: Pluto): 112–35.

Albright, Madeleine (1998) 'The Today Show'. Interview on NBC-TV. February 19.

Ali, Tariq and David Barsamian (2005) *Speaking of Empire and Resistance: Conversations with Tariq Ali* (New York and London: The New Press).

Amin, Samir (1977) *Imperialism and Unequal Development*. Trans. Alfred Ehrenfeld and Joan Pinkham (New York: Monthly Review Press).

——. (1988) *Eurocentrism*. Trans. Russell Moore (New York: Monthly Review Press).

——. (2000) 'The Challenge of Globalization'. *Postcolonialism: Critical Concepts in Literary and Cultural Studies*. Vol. 5. Ed. Diana Brydon (London and New York: Routledge): 1893–9.

——. (2004) 'The New Agrarian Issue: Three Billion Peasants Under Threat'. *Globalizing Resistance: The State of Struggle*. Eds François Polet and CETRI (London: Pluto): 226–40.

Amin, Shahid (1996) *Event, Metaphor, Memory: Chauri Chaura 1922–1992* (Delhi: Oxford University Press).

Anderson, Benedict (1983) *Imagined Communities: Reflections of the Origin and Spread of Nationalism* (London: Verso).

Anzaldúa, Gloria (1987) *Borderlands/La Frontera: The New Mestiza* (San Francisco: Spinsters/Aunt Lute).

Appadurai, Arjun (2000) 'Disjuncture and Difference in the Global Cultural Economy'. *Postcolonialism: Critical Concepts in Literary and Cultural Studies*, Vol. 5. Ed. Diana Brydon (London and New York: Routledge): 1801–23.

Arendt, Hannah (1962) *The Origins of Totalitarianism* (Ohio: Meridian).

——. (1968) *Imperialism* (New York: Harcourt Trade Publishers).

Aronowitz, Stanley (2003) 'Global Capital and Its Opponents'. *Implicating Empire: Globalization and Resistance in the 21st Century World Order*. Eds Stanley Aronowitz and Heather Gautney (New York: Basic Books): 179–95.

Aronowitz, Stanley and Heather Gautney, eds (2003) 'The Debate about Globalization: An Introduction'. *Implicating Empire: Globalization and Resistance in the 21st Century World Order* (New York: Basic Books): xi–xxx.

Ashcroft, Bill, Gareth Griffiths and Helen Tiffin (1989) *The Empire Writes Back: Theory and Practice in Post-Colonial Literatures* (London and New York: Routledge).

——. eds (1995) *The Post-Colonial Studies Reader* (London and New York: Routledge).

Barnet, Richard and John Cavanagh (1994) *Global Dreams: Imperial Corporations and the New World Order* (New York: Touchstone).

Bartolovich, Crystal (2000) 'Global Capital and Transnationalism'. *A Companion to Postcolonial Studies*. Eds Henry Schwarz and Sangeeta Ray (Oxford: Blackwell): 126–61.

——. (2002) 'Introduction: Marxism, Modernity, and Postcolonial Studies'. *Marxism, Modernity and Postcolonial Studies*. Eds Crystal Bartolovich and Neil Lazarus (Cambridge: Cambridge University Press): 1–17.

Baudrillard, Jean (1983) *In the Shadow of the Silent Majorities or, The End of the Social and Other Essays* (New York: Semiotext).

——. (1995) *The Gulf War Did Not Take Place*. Trans. Paul Patton (Sydney: Power Publications).

Bauman, Zygmunt (1998) *Globalization: The Human Consequences* (Cambridge: Polity).

Berlin, Isaiah (1976) *Vico and Herder: Two Studies in the History of Ideas* (London: Hogarth).

Bhabha, Homi K. (1990a) 'The Third Space: Interview with Homi Bhabha'. *Identity, Community, Culture, Difference*. Ed. Jonathan Rutherford (London: Lawrence and Wishart): 207–21.

——. ed. (1990b) *Nation and Narration* (London and New York: Routledge).

——. (1994) *The Location of Culture* (London and New York: Routledge).
Blauner, Bob (2001) *Still the Big News: Racial Oppression in America* (Philadelphia: Temple University Press).
Boehmer, Elleke (1995). *Colonial and Postcolonial Literature* (Oxford and New York: Oxford University Press).
Brah, Avtar (2002) 'Global Mobilities, Local Predicaments: Globalization and the Critical Imagination'. *Feminist Review*, Vol. 70: 30–45.
Brecher, Jeremy (2003) 'Globalization Today'. *Implicating Empire: Globalization and Resistance in the 21st Century World Order*. Eds Stanley Aronowitz and Heather Gautney (New York: Basic Books): 199–203.
Brennan, Timothy (1989) *Salman Rushdie and the Third World: Myths of the Nation* (Basingstoke and London: Macmillan).
Brückner, Martin (2003) 'The Critical Place of Empire in Early American Studies'. *American Literary History*, Vol. 15, No. 4: 809–21.
Brydon, Diana (2006) 'Is There a Politics of Postcoloniality?' *Postcolonial Text*, Vol. 2, No. 1: n.p. http://postcolonial.org/index.php/pct (accessed 7 May 2007).
Buell, Lawrence (1992) 'American Literary Emergence as a Postcolonial Phenomenon'. *American Literary History*, Vol. 4, No. 3: 411–42.
——. (1996) 'Are We Post-American Studies?' *Field Work: Sites in Literary and Cultural Studies*. Eds Marjorie Garber, Paul B. Franklin and Rebecca L. Walkowitz (New York and London: Routledge): 87–93.
——. (2000) 'Postcolonial Anxiety in Classic U.S. Literature'. *Postcolonial Theory and the United States: Race, Ethnicity and Literature*. Eds Amritjit Singh and Peter Schmidt (Jackson: University Press of Mississippi): 196–219.
Bush, George W. (2002) 'Securing Freedom's Triumph'. *New York Times*, 11 September: A. 33.
Cabral, Amilcar (1966) 'The Weapon of Theory: Address Delivered to the First Tricontinental Conference of the Peoples of Asia, Africa and Latin America, Havana'. http://www.marxists.org/subject/africa/cabral/1966/weapon-theory.htm (accessed 18 May 2010).
Callinicos, Alex (2003) 'Toni Negri in Perspective'. *Debating Empire*. Ed. Gopal Balakrishnan (London and New York: Verso): 121–43.
Césaire, Aimé (1972) 'An Interview with Aimé Césaire'. *Discourse on Colonialism*. Trans. Joan Pinkham (New York: Monthly Review Press): 65–79.
Chamberlain, John (1973) 'Nixon: A Keynesian With a Difference'. *The Evening Independent*, 30 January: 12.

Chandra, Bipan, Mridula Mukherjee, Aditya Mukherjee, K. N. Panikkar and Sucheta Mahajan (1989) *India's Struggle for Independence* (New Delhi: Penguin).

Chatterjee, Partha (1986) *Nationalist Thought and the Colonial World: A Derivative Discourse?* (London: Zed Books).

——. (1993a) *The Nation and Its Fragments: Colonial and Postcolonial Histories* (Princeton: Princeton University Press).

——. (1993b) 'The Need to Dissemble'. *Public Culture*, Vol. 6, No. 1: 55–64.

Cherniavsky, Eva (1996) 'Subaltern Studies in a U.S. Frame'. *boundary 2*, Vol. 23, No. 2: 85–110.

Childs, Peter and Patrick Williams (1997) *An Introduction to Post-Colonial Theory* (Essex: Pearson Education).

Chomsky, Noam (2000) *Rogue States: The Rule of Force in World Affairs* (London: Pluto).

——. (2001) *9-11* (New York: Seven Stories Press).

——. (2007) *Interventions* (San Francisco: City Lights Books).

Chrisman, Laura (2004) 'Nationalism and Postcolonial Studies'. *The Cambridge Companion to Postcolonial Literary Studies*. Ed. Neil Lazarus (Cambridge: Cambridge University Press): 183–98.

Conrad, Joseph (1995) *Heart of Darkness* (London: Penguin).

Davis, Horace B. (1978) *Toward a Marxist Theory of Nationalism* (New York and London: Monthly Review Press).

Debray, Régis (1977) 'Marxism and the National Question'. *New Left Review*, Vol. 105: 25–41.

Devi, Rassundari (1999) *Amar Jiban* (My Life). Trans. Enakshi Chatterjee (Calcutta: Writers Workshop).

Dirlik, Arif (1994) 'The Postcolonial Aura: Third World Capitalism in the Age of Global Capitalism', *Critical Inquiry*, Vol. 20: 328–56.

'Disinvestment and Privatisation'. *Public Enterprises Survey 2005–06*, Vol. 1: 100–8. http://dpe.nic.in/survey0506/vol1/vol1ch6.pdf (accessed 15 February 2009).

Ditz, Jason (2009) 'Obama Vows US Military Will Remain World's Strongest'. *Antiwar.com*. 13 March. http://news.antiwar.com (accessed 23 September 2009).

Eagleton, Terry (1998) 'Postcolonialism and "Postcolonialism"'. *Interventions: International Journal of Postcolonial Studies*, Vol. 1, No. 1: 24–6.

Edwards, Brian T. (2003) 'Preposterous Encounters: Interrupting American Studies with the (Post)Colonial, or *Casablanca* in the American Century'. *Comparative Studies of South Asia, Africa and the Middle East*, Vol. 23, Nos. 1 and 2: 70–86.

El Sa'adawi, Nawal (2007) *Woman at Point Zero* (London: Zed).

Eriksen, Thomas Hylland (1993) *Ethnicity and Nationalism: Anthropological Perspectives* (London: Pluto).
Faludi, Susan (2007) *The Terror Dream, Fear and Fantasy in Post-9/11 America* (New York: Metropolitan Books).
Fanon, Frantz (1986) *Black Skin, White Masks* (London: Pluto).
——. (1967) *The Wretched of the Earth*. Trans. Constance Farrington (Harmondsworth: Penguin).
Fergusson, Niall (2001) 'Welcome the New Imperialism'. *Guardian*, 31 October.
'For a Few Dollars More' (2006) *People's Democracy: Weekly Organ of the Communist Part of India (Marxist)*, Vol. 30, No. 3, 15 January.
Frankenberg, Ruth and Lata Mani (2000) 'Crosscurrents, Crosstalk: Race, "Postcoloniality" and the Politics of Location'. *Postcolonialism: Critical Concepts in Literary and Cultural Studies*, Vol. 5. Ed. Diana Brydon (London and New York: Routledge): 1846–65.
Friedman, Thomas L. (2003) 'A War for Oil'. *New York Times*, 5 January.
——. (2000) *The Lexus and the Olive Tree* (New York: Anchor).
——. (2005) *The World is Flat* (New York: Farrar, Straus and Giroux).
Galeano, Eduardo (1997) *Open Veins of Latin America: Five Centuries of the Pillage of a Continent* (New York: Monthly Review Press).
Garrett, Geoffrey (2004) 'Partisan Politics in the Global Economy'. *The Globalization Reader*. Eds Frank J. Lechner and John Boli (Oxford: Blackwell): 231–9.
Gikandi, Simon (2001) 'Globalization and the Claims of Postcoloniality'. *The South Atlantic Quarterly*, Vol. 100, No. 3: 627–58.
——. (2004) 'Poststructuralism and Postcolonial Discourse'. *The Cambridge Companion to Postcolonial Literary Studies*. Ed. Neil Lazarus (Cambridge: Cambridge University Press): 97–119.
Giles, Paul (2004) 'Response to the Presidential Address to the American Studies Association, Hartford, Connecticut, 17 October 2003'. *American Quarterly*, Vol. 56, No. 1: 19–24.
Gilroy, Paul (1993) *The Black Atlantic: Modernity and Double Consciousness* (London: Verso).
——. (2004) *After Empire: Melancholia or Convivial Culture?* (Oxfordshire: Routledge).
Giroux, Henry A. (2010) 'Winter in America: Democracy Gone Rogue'. http://www.truthout.org/winter-america-democracy-gone-rogue57353 (accessed 2 May 2010).
Glasberg, Elena (2000) 'On the Road with Chrysler: From Nation to Virtual Empire'. *Postcolonial America*. Ed. C. Richard King (Urbana and Chicago: University of Illinois Press): 154–70.
Gopal, Sangita (2003) 'Hindu Buying/Hindu Being: Hindutva Online and the Commodity Logic of Cultural Nationalism'. *South Asian Review*, Vol. 24, No. 1: 161–79.

Graeber, David (2003) 'The Globalization Movement and the New Left'. *Implicating Empire: Globalization and Resistance in the 21st Century World Order*. Eds Stanley Aronowitz and Heather Gautney (New York: Basic Books): 325–38.

Griffiths, Gareth (1996) 'Representation and Production: Issues of Control in Post-colonial Cultures'. Eds Harish Trivedi and Meenakshi Mukherjee, *Interrogating Post-colonialism: Theory, Text and Context* (Shimla: Indian Institute of Advanced Studies): 21–36.

Hall, Stuart (1990) 'Cultural Identity and Diaspora'. *Identity, Community, Culture, Difference*. Ed. Jonathan Rutherford (London: Lawrence and Wishart): 222–37.

——. (1991) 'Old and New Identities, Old and New Ethnicities'. *Culture, Globalization and the World-System*. Ed. Anthony D. King (Hampshire and London: Macmillan): 41–68.

——. (1996) 'When was "the Post-Colonial?" Thinking at the Limit'. *The Post-Colonial Question: Common Skies, Divided Horizons*. Eds Iain Chambers and Lidia Curti (London and New York: Routledge): 242–60.

Hallward, Peter (2001) *Absolutely Postcolonial: Writing Between the Singular and the Specific* (Manchester and New York: Manchester University Press).

Hardt, Michael (2002) 'Today's Bandung'. *New Left Review*, Vol. 14: 112–18.

Hardt, Michael and Antonio Negri (2000) *Empire* (Cambridge, MA: Harvard University Press).

——. (2003) 'Globalization and Democracy'. *Implicating Empire: Globalization and Resistance in the 21st Century World Order*. Eds Stanley Aronowitz and Heather Gautney (New York: Basic Books): 109–21.

Harvey, David (2003) *The New Imperialism* (Oxford: Oxford University Press).

Hershberg, Eric and Fred Rosen, eds (2006) *Latin America After Neoliberalism: Turning the Tide in the 21st Century?* (New York and London: The New Press).

Hoogvelt, Ankie (1997) *Globalisation and the Postcolonial World: The New Political Economy of Development* (London: Macmillan).

Hutchinson, John and Anthony D. Smith, eds (1994) *Nationalism* (Oxford: Oxford University Press).

Ignatieff, Michael (2002) 'Nation-Building Lite'. *New York Times Magazine*, 28 July: 1–11.

Jameson, Fredric (2000) 'Globalization and Political Strategy'. *New Left Review*, Vol. 4: 49–68.

Jefferess, David, Julie McGonegal and Sabine Mitz (2006) 'Introduction: The Politics of Postcoloniality', *Postcolonial Text*, Vol. 2, No. 1: n.p. http://postcolonial.org/index.php/pct (accessed 7 May 2007).

Jennar, Roul-Marc (2004) 'New Powers, New Counter-Powers'. *Globalizing Resistance: The State of Struggle*. Eds François Polet and CETRI (London: Pluto): 289–93.

John, Mary E. (1999) 'Feminisms and Internationalisms: A Response from India'. *Feminisms and Internationalism*. Eds Mrinalini Sinha, Donna Guy and Angela Woollacott (Oxford: Blackwell): 195–204.

Johnson, Chalmers (2004) *The Sorrows of Empire* (London: Verso).

——. (2009) 'Three Good Reasons to Liquidate our Empire'. *Tomdispatch.Com*, 31 July. http://www.alternet.org/world (accessed 27 December 2009).

Jowitt, Ken (1992) *New World Disorder: The Leninist Extinction* (Berkeley and Los Angeles: University of California Press).

Kaplan, Amy (1993) '"Left Alone with America": The Absence of Empire in the Study of American Culture'. *Cultures of United States Imperialism*. Eds Amy Kaplan and Donald E. Pease (Durham, NC: Duke University Press): 3–21.

——. (2004) 'Violent Belongings and the Question of Empire Today'. *American Quarterly*, Vol. 56, No. 1: 1–18.

Kaplan, Amy and Donald E. Pease, eds (1993) *Cultures of United States Imperialism* (Durham, NC: Duke University Press).

Kapur, Geeta (1990) 'Contemporary Cultural Practice: Some Polemical Categories'. *Social Scientist*, Vol. 18, No. 3: 49–59.

Kedourie, Elie, ed. (1970) 'Introduction'. *Nationalism in Asia and Africa* (London: Weidenfeld and Nicolson): 1–152.

Khilnani, Sunil (1997) *The Idea of India* (London: Hamish Hamilton).

King, C. Richard, ed. (2000) 'Introduction'. *Postcolonial America* (Urbana and Chicago: University of Illinois Press): 1–17.

Klein, Naomi (2001) 'Squatters in White Overalls'. *Guardian*, 8 June.

——. (2002a) *Fences and Windows: Dispatches from the Front Lines of the Globalization Debate* (London: Flamingo).

——. (2002b) 'Interview with Lyn Thomas'. *Feminist Review*, Vol. 70: 46–56.

Kohn, Hans (1944) *The Idea of Nationalism: A Study in Its Origins and Background* (New York: Macmillan).

Koundoura, Maria (1989) 'Naming Gayatri Spivak'. *Stanford Humanities Review*, Vol. 1: 84–97.

Kumar, Radha (1993) *The History of Doing: An Illustrated Account of Movements for Women's Rights and Feminism in India 1800–1990* (London and New York: Verso).

Lakshman, Narayan (2010) 'Too Much Representation, Too Little Democracy'. *The Hindu*, 4 April.

Lazarus, Neil (1997) 'Transnationalism and the Alleged Death of the Nation-State'. *Cultural Readings of Imperialism: Edward Said and the Gravity of History*. Eds Keith Ansell-Pearson, Benita Parry and Judith Squires (New York: St Martin's Press): 28–48.

——. (1999) *Nationalism and Cultural Practice in the Postcolonial World* (Cambridge: Cambridge University Press).

——. (2002) 'The Fetish of "the West" in Postcolonial Theory'. *Marxism, Modernity and Postcolonial Studies*. Eds Crystal Bartolovich and Neil Lazarus (Cambridge: Cambridge University Press): 43–64.

Lechner, Frank J. and John Boli, eds (2004) 'Introduction'. *The Globalization Reader*. (Oxford: Blackwell): 211–13.

Lewis, R. W. B. (1955) *The American Adam: Innocence and Tradition in the Nineteenth Century* (Chicago: University of Chicago Press).

List, Friedrich (1856) *National System of Political Economy*. Trans. G. A. Matile (United States: J. B. Lippincott).

Llana, Sara Miller (2009) 'Where has Chávez Taken Venezuela?' *Christian Science Monitor*, 2 February. http://www.csmonitor.com/World/Americas/2009/0202/p01s03-woam.html (accessed 26 May 2010).

Loomba, Ania (1993) 'Dead Women Tell No Tales: Issues of Female Subjectivity, Subaltern Agency and Tradition in Colonial and Post-colonial Writings on Widow Immolation in India', *History Workshop Journal*, Vol. 36: 209–27.

——. (1998a) *Colonialism/Postcolonialism* (London and New York: Routledge).

——. (1998b) 'Postcolonialism – or Postcolonial Studies'. *Interventions: International Journal of Postcolonial Studies*, Vol. 1, No. 1: 39–42.

López, Alfred J. (2001) *Posts and Pasts: A Theory of Postcolonialism* (New York: State University of New York Press).

Lundestad, Geir (1986) 'Empire by Invitation? The United States and Western Europe, 1945–52'. *Journal of Peace Research*, Vol. 23, No. 3: 263–77.

Luxemburg, Rosa (1951) *The Accumulation of Capital*. Trans. Agnes Schwarzschild (New York: Monthly Review Press).

McClintock, Anne (1991) '"No Longer in a Future Heaven": Women and Nationalism in South Africa'. *Transition*, Vol. 51: 104–23.

——. (1993) 'The Angel of Progress: Pitfalls of the term "Post-Colonialism"'. *Colonial Discourse and Post-Colonial Theory*. Eds Patrick Williams and Laura Chrisman (New York and London: Harvester Wheatsheaf): 291–304.

McLeod, John (2000) *Beginning Postcolonialism* (Manchester and New York: Manchester University Press).

McQuillan, Martin, Graeme Macdonald, Robin Purves and Stephen Thomson, eds (1999) *Post-Theory: New Directions in Criticism* (Edinburgh: Edinburgh University Press).

Manuel, Frank E., ed. (1968) *Reflections on the Philosophy of the History of Mankind* (Chicago: University of Chicago Press).

Marable, Manning (2003) '9/11: Racism in a Time of Terror'. *Implicating Empire: Globalization and Resistance in the 21st Century World Order*. Eds Stanley Aronowitz and Heather Gautney (New York: Basic Books): 3–14.

Marcos, Subcomandante (1997) 'The Fourth World War has Begun'. *Nepantla: Views from South*, Vol. 2, No. 3: 559–72.

Marx, Karl and Friedrich Engels (1967) *The Communist Manifesto* (London: Penguin).

Mayo, Katherine (1927) *Mother India* (London: Jonathan Cape).

Mbembe, Achille (2000) 'Provisional Notes on the Postcolony'. *Postcolonialism: Critical Concepts in Literary and Cultural Studies*. Vol. 1. Ed. Diana Brydon (London and New York: Routledge): 134–74.

Meiksins Wood, Ellen (2003) 'A Manifesto for Global Capital?' *Debating Empire*. Ed. Gopal Balakrishnan (London and New York: Verso): 61–82.

Menchú, Rigoberta (1984) *I, Rigoberta Menchú* (London: Verso).

Mertes, Tom (2003) 'Grass-Roots Globalism'. *Debating Empire*. Ed. Gopal Balakrishnan (London and New York: Verso): 144–54.

Mestrum, Francine (2004) 'The World Social Forum: A Democratic Alternative'. *Globalizing Resistance: The State of Struggle*. Eds François Polet and CETRI (London: Pluto): 188–205.

Mill, John Stuart (1965) *Principles of Political Economy with Some of Their Applications to Social Philosophy*. Book III (London: Routledge and Kegan Paul).

Miller, Perry (1956) *Errand into the Wilderness* (Cambridge, MA: Belknap).

——. (1963) *Nature's Nation* (Cambridge, MA: Belknap).

Mishra, Vijay (1996) 'The Diasporic Imaginary: Theorizing the Indian Diaspora'. *Textual Practice*, Vol. 10, No. 3: 421–47.

Miyoshi, Masao (1997) 'Sites of Resistance in the Global Economy'. *Cultural Readings of Imperialism: Edward Said and the Gravity of History*. Eds Keith Ansell-Pearson, Benita Parry and Judith Squires (New York: St Martin's Press): 49–66.

——. (2000) 'A Borderless World? From Colonialism to Transnationalism and the Decline of the Nation-State'. *Postcolonialism: Critical Concepts in Literary and Cultural Studies*. Vol. 5. Ed. Diana Brydon (London and New York: Routledge): 1867–92.

Moore-Gilbert, Bart (1997) *Postcolonial Theory: Contexts, Practices, Politics* (London: Verso).

Mostern, Kenneth (2000) 'Postcolonialism after W. E. B. DuBois'. *Postcolonial Theory and the United States: Race, Ethnicity and Literature*. Eds Amritjit Singh and Peter Schmidt (Jackson: University Press of Mississippi): 258–76.

Mukherjee, Arun P. (1996) 'Interrogating Postcolonialism: Some Uneasy Conjunctures'. *Interrogating Post-colonialism: Theory, Text and Context*. Eds Harish Trivedi and Meenakshi Mukherjee (Shimla: Indian Institute of Advanced Studies): 13–20.

Mukherjee, Meenakshi (1996) 'Interrogating Post-colonialism'. *Interrogating Post-colonialism: Theory, Text and Context*. Eds Harish Trivedi and Meenakshi Mukherjee (Shimla: Indian Institute of Advanced Studies): 3–11.

Nandy, Ashis (1994) *The Illegitimacy of Nationalism: Rabindranath Tagore and the Politics of the Self* (Delhi: Oxford University Press).

Nehru, Jawaharlal (1947) 'Speech Delivered to the Constituent Assembly of India, New Delhi, August 14, 1947'. 'Great Speeches of the Twentieth Century'. *Guardian*, 1 May 2007.

Nigam, Aditya (2006) 'Das Kapital in Buddha's Bengal?' *Tehelka: The People's Paper*, 29 January: 19.

Nkrumah, Kwame (1965) 'Neo-Colonialism, the Last Stage of Imperialism'. http://www.assatashakur.org/forum/liberation-strategy/31083-neo-colonialism-last-stage-imperialism-kwame-nkrumah-1965-a.html (accessed 14 March 2010).

Notes from Nowhere, ed. (2003) *We are Everywhere: The Irresistible Rise of Global Anticapitalism* (London and New York: Verso).

O'Brien, Susie (2000) 'New Postnational Narratives, Old American Dreams; or, The Problem with Coming-of-Age Stories'. *Postcolonial America*. Ed. C. Richard King (Urbana and Chicago: University of Illinois Press): 65–79.

Ohmae, Kenichi (2004) 'The End of the Nation State'. *The Globalization Reader*. Eds Frank J. Lechner and John Boli (Oxford: Blackwell): 214–18.

Oxfam (2002) 'Rigged Rules and Double Standards: Trade, Globalisation and the Fight Against Poverty' (London: Oxfam).

Panitch, Leo and Sam Gindin (2003) 'Gems and Baubles in Empire'. *Debating Empire*. Ed. Gopal Balakrishnan (London and New York: Verso): 52–9.

——. (2004) *Global Capitalism and American Empire* (London: Merlin).

Paranjape, Makarand (1996) 'Coping with Post-Colonialism'. *Interrogating Post-colonialism: Theory, Text and Context*. Eds Harish Trivedi and Meenakshi Mukherjee (Shimla: Indian Institute of Advanced Studies): 37–47.

Parker, Andrew, Mary Russo, Doris Sommer and Patricia Yaeger, eds (1992) *Nationalisms and Sexualities* (New York and London: Routledge).

Parry, Benita (1987) 'Problems in Current Theories of Colonial Discourse', *Oxford Literary Review*, Vol. 9, Nos. 1–2 (1987): 27–58.

——. (2002) 'Directions and Dead Ends in Postcolonial Studies'. *Relocating Postcolonialism*. Eds David Theo Goldberg and Ato Quayson (Oxford: Blackwell): 66–81.

——. (2004a) 'The Institutionalisation of Postcolonial Studies'. *The Cambridge Companion to Postcolonial Literary Studies*. Ed. Neil Lazarus (Cambridge: Cambridge University Press): 66–80.

——. (2004b) *Postcolonial Studies: A Materialist Critique* (London and New York: Routledge).

Pease, Donald E., ed. (1994) *National Identities and Post-Americanist Narratives* (Durham, NC and London: Duke University Press).

——. (2000) 'US Imperialism: Global Dominance Without Colonies'. *A Companion to Postcolonial Studies*. Eds Henry Schwarz and Sangeeta Ray (Oxford: Blackwell): 203–20.

Phalkey, Jahnavi (1999) 'Right-wing Mobilization of Women in India: *Hindutva's* Willing Performers'. *Women, Globalization and Fragmentation in the Developing World*. Eds Haleh Afshar and Stephanie Barrientos (Basingstoke and London: Macmillan): 38–53.

Plamenatz, John (1976) 'Two Types of Nationalism'. *Nationalism: The Nature and Evolution of an Idea*. Ed. Eugene Kamenka (London: Edward Arnold): 23–36.

Prakash, Gyan (1990) 'Writing Post-Orientalist Histories of the Third World: Perspectives from Indian Historiography'. *Comparative Studies in Society and History*, Vol. 32: 383–408.

Radhakrishnan, R. (1992) 'Nationalism, Gender, and the Narrative of Identity'. *Nationalisms and Sexualities*. Eds Andrew Parker, Mary Russo, Doris Sommer, and Patricia Yaeger (New York and London: Routledge): 77–95.

Rai, Shirin M. (1999) 'Fractioned States and Negotiated Boundaries: Gender and Law in India'. *Women, Globalization and Fragmentation in the Developing World*. Eds Haleh Afshar and Stephanie Barrientos (Hampshire and London: Macmillan): 18–37.

Raina, Vinod (2004) 'Political Diversity, Common Purpose: Social Movements in India'. *Globalizing Resistance: The State of Struggle*. Eds François Polet and CETRI (London: Pluto): 3–14.

Raschka, Marilyn (1995) 'India's Right-Wing BJP Positioning for 1996 Elections'. http://www.wrmea.com/backissues/1095/9510050.htm (accessed 26 May 2010).

Reuters (2004) 'Israel to Press on With Wall'. *Indian Express*, 22 July: 18.

Riverbend (2006) *Baghdad Burning: A Young Woman's Diary From a War Zone* (New Delhi: Women Unlimited).
Rohter, Larry (2002) 'Jet Purchase Splits Brazil: New Leader Wants Voice'. *New York Times*, 29 November.
Rowe, John Carlos (2000a) *Literary Culture and U.S. Imperialism: From the Revolution to World War II* (Oxford: Oxford University Press).
——. (2002a) *The New American Studies* (Minneapolis and London: University of Minnesota Press).
——. (2002b) 'Postnationalism, Globalism, and the New American Studies'. *The Future of American Studies.* Eds Donald E. Pease and Robyn Wiegman (Durham, NC and London: Duke University Press): 167–82.
——. (2004) 'Edward Said and American Studies'. *American Quarterly*, Vol. 56, No. 1: 33–47.
——. ed. (2000b) *Post-Nationalist American Studies* (Berkeley and Los Angeles: University of California Press).
Roy, Arundhati (1999) *The Greater Common Good* (Bombay: India Book Distributors).
——. (2001) *Power Politics* (Cambridge, MA: South End Press).
——. (2004) *The Ordinary Person's Guide to Empire* (London: Flamingo).
——. (2009) *Listening to Grass-Hoppers: Field Notes on Democracy* (New Delhi: Penguin).
Rushdie, Salman (1980) *Midnight's Children* (New York: Avon).
Rushdie, Salman and Elizabeth West (1997) *The Vintage Book of Indian Writing: 1947–1997* (London: Vintage).
Said, Edward W. (1978) *Orientalism* (London: Routledge).
——. (1993) *Culture and Imperialism* (London: Chatto and Windus).
——. (1995) 'Afterword'. *Orientalism* (New Delhi: Penguin).
——. (2001) 'The Events and Aftermath'. *Observer*, September 16.
San Juan, Jr., E. (1998) *Beyond Postcolonial Theory* (New York: St Martin's Press).
Sardar, Ziauddin (1998) *Postmodernism and the Other: The New Imperialism of Western Culture* (London: Pluto).
Sardar, Ziauddin and Merryl Wyn Davies (2002) *Why do People Hate America?* (Cambridge: Icon).
Sarkar, Tanika (2001) *Hindu Wife, Hindu Nation: Community, Religion and Cultural Nationalism* (New Delhi: Permanent Black).
Sartre, Jean-Paul (1967) 'Preface'. *The Wretched of the Earth*. By Frantz Fanon. Trans. Constance Farrington (Harmondsworth: Penguin).
Schueller, Malini Johar (1998) *U.S. Orientalisms: Race, Nation, and Gender in Literature, 1790–1890* (Ann Arbor: University of Michigan Press).

——. (2004) 'Postcolonial American Studies'. *American Literary History*, Vol. 16, No. 1: 162–75.

Schueller, Malini Johar and Edward Watts (2003) 'Introduction: Theorizing Early American Studies and Postcoloniality'. *Messy Beginnings: Postcoloniality and Early American Studies*. Eds Malini Johar Schueller and Edward Watts (New Brunswick, New Jersey and London: Rutgers University Press): 1–25.

Schwarz, Henry (2000) 'Mission Impossible: Introducing Postcolonial Studies in the US Academy'. *A Companion to Postcolonial Studies*. Eds Henry Schwarz and Sangeeta Ray (Oxford: Blackwell): 1–20.

Schwarz, Henry and Sangeeta Ray, eds (2000) *A Companion to Postcolonial Studies* (Oxford: Blackwell).

Sen, Amartya (2002) Preface to 'Rigged Rules and Double Standards: Trade, Globalisation and the Fight Against Poverty' (London: Oxfam).

Sethi, Rumina (1999) *Myths of the Nation: National Identity and Literary Representation* (Oxford: Clarendon).

——. (2007) 'New Perceptions of Nationalist Politics: Reconsidering Motherhood'. *Focus India: Postcolonial Narratives of the Nation*. Eds Meenakshi Mukherjee, Harish Trivedi, C. Vijayasree and T. Vijay Kumar (New Delhi: Pencraft International): 18–33.

Sharpe, Jenny (2000a) 'Is the United States Postcolonial? Transnationalism, Immigration, and Race'. *Postcolonial America*. Ed. C. Richard King (Urbana and Chicago: University of Illinois Press): 103–21.

——. (2000b) 'Postcolonial Studies in the House of US Multiculturalism'. *A Companion to Postcolonial Studies*. Eds Henry Schwarz and Sangeeta Ray (Oxford: Blackwell): 112–25.

Shiva, Vandana (1989) *Staying Alive: Women, Ecology and Development* (London: Zed Books).

——. (2002) 'Export at any Cost: Oxfam's Free Trade Recipe for the Third World'. http://www.zcommunications.org/export-at-any-cost-by-vandana2-shiva (accessed 8 March 2007).

——. (2005) *Globalization's New Wars: Seed, Water and Life Forms* (New Delhi: Women Unlimited).

Shohat, Ella (1992) 'Notes on the Post-Colonial', *Social Text*, Vols. 31–2: 99–113.

Singh, Amritjit and Peter Schmidt (2000) 'On the Borders Between US Studies and Postcolonial Theory'. *Postcolonial Theory and the United States: Race, Ethnicity and Literature*. Eds Amritjit Singh and Peter Schmidt (Jackson: University Press of Mississippi): 4–69.

Sinha, Mrinalini (2006) *Spectres of Mother India: The Global Restructuring of an Empire* (Durham, NC: Duke University Press).

Sivanandan, Tamara (2004) 'Anticolonialism, National Liberation, and Postcolonial Nation Formation'. *The Cambridge Companion to Postcolonial Literary Studies*. Ed. Neil Lazarus (Cambridge: Cambridge University Press): 41–65.

Slemon, Stephen (1994) 'The Scramble for Post-Colonialism'. *De-Scribing Empire: Post-Colonialism and Textuality*. Eds Chris Tiffin and Alan Lawson (London and New York: Routledge): 15–32.

Smith, Anthony D. (1991) *National Identity* (Harmondsworth: Penguin).

Spivak, Gayatri Chakravorty (1984) 'The Rani of Sirmur'. Ed. Francis Barker et al., *Europe and Its Others: Proceedings of the Essex Conference on the Sociology of Literature*, Vol. 1 (Colchester: University of Essex, 1985): 128–51.

——. (1988a) 'A Literary Representation of the Subaltern: A Woman's Text from the Third World'. *In Other Worlds: Essays in Cultural Politics* (London and New York: Routledge): 241–68.

——. (1988b) 'Can the Subaltern Speak?' Eds Cary Nelson and Lawrence Grossberg, *Marxism and the Interpretation of Culture* (Urbana: University of Illinois): 271–313.

——. (1989) 'Who Claims Alterity?' *Remaking History*. Eds Barbara Kruger and Phil Mariani (Seattle: Bay Press): 269–92.

——. (1990) *The Post-Colonial Critic: Interviews, Strategies, Dialogues*. Ed. Sarah Harasym (London and New York: Routledge).

——. (1992) 'Asked to Talk About Myself...'. *Third Text*, Vol. 19: 9–18.

——. (1993) 'Woman in Difference'. *Outside in the Teaching Machine* (London and New York: Routledge): 77–95.

——. (1995) *Imaginary Maps: Three Stories by Mahasweta Devi* (London: Routledge).

Sprinker, Michael (1993) 'The National Question: Said, Ahmad, Jameson'. *Public Culture*, Vo. 6, No. 1: 3–29.

Stiglitz, Joseph E. (2002) *Globalization and its Discontents* (New York: W. W. Norton).

——. (2004) 'Globalism's Discontents'. *The Globalization Reader*. Eds Frank J. Lechner and John Boli (Oxford: Blackwell): 200–7.

——. (2010) *Freefall: Free Markets and the Sinking of the Global Economy* (London: Allen Lane).

Strange, Susan (2004) 'The Declining Authority of States'. *The Globalization Reader*. Eds Frank J. Lechner and John Boli (Oxford: Blackwell): 219–24.

Stratton, Jon (2000) 'The Beast of the Apocalypse: The Postcolonial Experience of the United States'. *Postcolonial America*. Ed. C. Richard King (Urbana and Chicago: University of Illinois Press): 21–63.

Szeman, Imre (2003) *Zones of Instability: Literature, Postcolonialism, and the Nation* (Baltimore and London: Johns Hopkins University Press).

Tagore, Rabindranath (1918) *Nationalism* (London: Macmillan).

——. (2002) *Letters to a Friend: Rabindranath Tagore's Letters to C. F. Andrews* (New Delhi: Rupa).

Tarlo, Emma (1996) *Clothing Matters: Dress and Identity in India* (London: Hurst).

Tharu, Susie and K. Lalita, eds (1995) *Women Writing in India*, 2 vols. (Delhi: Oxford University Press).

Tohidi, Nayereh (1991) 'Gender and Islamic Fundamentalism: Feminist Politics in Iran'. *Third World Women and the Politics of Feminism*. Eds Chandra Talpade Mohanty, Ann Russo, and Lourdes Torres (Bloomington and Indianapolis: Indiana University Press): 251–67.

Trivedi, Harish (1993) *Colonial Transactions: English Literature and India* (Calcutta: Papyrus).

——. (2010) 'India, America and World Literature'. Keynote Address. International Conference on Contemporary Issues: Literature and Culture since 1980. Panjab University, Chandigarh. 25 February.

Tyler, Patrick E. (2003) 'A New Power in the Streets'. *New York Times*, 17 February.

Wallerstein, Immanuel (1983) *Historical Capitalism* (London: Verso).

Werbner, Pnina and Tariq Modood, eds (1997) *Debating Cultural Hybridity: Multi-Cultural Identities and the Politics of Anti-Racism* (London: Zed).

Williams, Patrick and Laura Chrisman, eds (1993) *Colonial Discourse and Post-Colonial Theory: A Reader* (Hertfordshire: Harvester Wheatsheaf).

Williams, Raymond (1983) *Keywords: A Vocabulary of Culture and Society* (London: Flamingo).

Young, Robert J. C. (1992) *White Mythologies: Writing History and the West* (London: Routledge).

——. (1995) *Colonial Desire: Hybridity in Theory, Culture and Race* (London and New York: Routledge).

——. (1998) 'Ideologies of the Postcolonial'. *Interventions: International Journal of Postcolonial Studies*, Vol. 1, No. 1: 4–8.

——. (2001) *Postcolonialism: An Historical Introduction* (Oxford: Blackwell).

Žižek, Slavoj (2009) *First as Tragedy, Then as Farce* (London: Verso).

Zutshi, Somnath (1993) 'Women, Nation and the Outsider in Contemporary Hindi Cinema'. *Interrogating Modernity: Culture and Colonialism in India*. Eds Tejaswini Niranjana, P. Sudhir and Vivek Dhareshwar (Calcutta: Seagull): 83–142.

INDEX